Not Eden

Not Eden

Spiritual Life Writing for this World

Heather Walton

scm press

© Heather Walton 2015

Published in 2015 by SCM Press
Editorial office
3rd Floor, Invicta House
108-114 Golden Lane,
London EC1Y 0TG.

SCM Press is an imprint of Hymns Ancient & Modern Ltd
(a registered charity)
13A Hellesdon Park Road
Norwich NR6 5DR, UK

www.scmpress.co.uk

All rights reserved. No part of this publication may be reproduced,
stored in a retrieval system, or transmitted,
in any form or by any means, electronic, mechanical,
photocopying or otherwise, without the prior permission of
the publisher, SCM Press.

The Author has asserted her right under the Copyright,
Designs and Patents Act, 1988,
to be identified as the Author of this Work

British Library Cataloguing in Publication data

A catalogue record for this book is available
from the British Library

978-0-334-05379-8

Typeset by Manila Typesetting Company
Printed and bound by
CPI Group (UK) Ltd, Croydon

For Wendy and for John

Contents

Acknowledgements   ix

Part 1   For This World: The Challenges of Spiritual Life Writing   1

    Introduction   3
  1   Ancient Practice, New Purpose   7
  2   Locating the Sacred   21
  3   Craft and Creativity   32

Bibliography   43

Part 2   Not Eden: A Work of Spiritual Life Writing   49

  1   Growth   51
  2   Blossoms   57
  3   Blight   62
  4   Rootbuds   66
  5   Nature and Grace   73
  6   The Fruit You Shall Not Eat   79
  7   White and Red Roses   86
  8   Little Flowers   91
  9   Fruit of the Spirit   96
10   Generation   101

11	Growing Wild	107
12	Bindweed	112
13	Green Stones	119
14	Lily	123
15	Bearing Fruit	128
16	The Flowering Rod	135

Questions for Reading Groups Using the Book   138

Resources for Writers   140

Acknowledgements

Not Eden went through a number of rewritings before attaining its present form. I am very grateful for those who helped me along the way at various stages of its development.

First, I would like to thank those close friends from Manchester who supported me while I wrestled with infertility, and first started to try and write about it. I am grateful to Ann Jones, Jane Hodges, Ian Stephens, Stuart Robbins, Linda Balfe, Alec Mitchell, Ian Parker, Erica Burman, Elaine Graham, Frances Ward, Susan Durber and Richard Kidd.

It was when I began to study Creative Writing at Goldsmiths that a revised version of this text began to take clearer shape. I owe a great deal to the teaching and supervision I received during my studies. Particular thanks to Maura Dooley and Blake Morrison. Also to John Walton and Louise Petre, as well as Jane Hodges and Bob Gilbert, who opened their homes to me on my frequent trips to London.

That this work was eventually completed is thanks to the encouragement of friends, colleagues and students who affirmed my conviction that life writing had a significant role to play in theological reflection. Once again, I would like to express my gratitude to my companions in the Centre for Literature, Theology and the Arts at the University of Glasgow and my colleagues in the Doctorate in Practical Theology Consortium. Particular thanks are due to Elizabeth Anderson and Anna Fisk – for continually encouraging me to keep up with them. Alison Jasper, Leah Robinson, Bonnie Miller-McLemore, Wendy Hesse and Fiona Darroch sustained me with their friendship and wise advice. My mother, Hazel Walton, my sister, Helen Baston, and my daughter, Maia Walton, have been gracious and perceptive readers of my work. Joan Mulheron gave the support that kept me sane enough to write. Anna Fisk and Ioulia Kolovou provided significant research assistance. Natalie Watson has been a courageous and creative editor. This work would not have been born without her help.

Throughout each stage of writing this book my partner, Reinier Holst, has been loving and remarkably patient. To him I owe my whole world.

Glasgow
Lent, 2015

PART I

For This World: The Challenges of Spiritual Life Writing

Introduction

Spiritual life writing spins threads between the sacred and the everyday. This living tradition is one of the most effective resources we have for generating radical visions out of the earthy, commonplace material of lived experience.

This work sets out to identify the methods and forms of spiritual life writing that are appropriate and meaningful within contemporary culture. To do so I shall draw upon my own practice as a writer, my work as an engaged academic, and my commitment to a faith that is rooted in daily life. I shall also explore the traditions of spiritual autobiography in the conviction that these should not be discarded – but rather radically re-formed in order to speak anew in today's context. Mercifully this is a short(ish) 'invitation to exploration', not a treatise on spiritual writing. I thus have good reason to be polemical: in order to make points directly and without apology, partial in order to highlight those aspects of the topic that seem to be most significant, and political. The text unashamedly assumes that spiritual writing 'for this world' will not be closed, conventional and regulatory. I am seeking forms of writing that are both open to the Spirit and responsive to the challenges we face in seeking the common good.

It is my hope that what follows will be useful to both the readers and practitioners of spiritual life writing. Reading this literature has provided a means of making imaginative spiritual journeys for many centuries. There is much to be gained by accompanying someone 'on the way'. Engaging with the critical questions raised here should make your travelling dialogues livelier and richer. But this work is most particularly for those who are setting out to write spiritual self-narratives as part of a personal quest, as a form of disciplined reflection, or because they have been encouraged to do so as part of a training or formation programme. It is my intention both to complicate and simplify the writing process. I think that the complex challenges that confront spiritual writers are not easy to resolve – although wrestling with them has the potential to generate some richly rewarding spiritual insights. To simplify things I have sought to straightforwardly present some matters of craft and style that are particularly significant when writing about the self and writing about the sacred.

Before proceeding any further, I acknowledge that at this point I could justifiably be expected to ground this work on a definition of spirituality – or at least attempt to say exactly what it is that makes certain forms of life writing 'spiritual'. Although 'spirituality' is now very commonly referred to in diverse spheres of life, from education to ecology, there is no widely accepted definition of the term and its usage differs according to context. In the United States, for example, it is rather more closely linked to religion than it is in the United Kingdom. Here it often refers broadly to a person's sense of meaning in life, connectedness (to people, nature, and/or the divine) and the quest to reach beyond the self to something that transcends the immediate and personal – regardless of religious affiliation. My friends John Swinton and Stephen Pattison (2010) have persuasively argued that part of the usefulness of the term lies in its slippery adaptability and that too tight a definition may be counterproductive. Being a rather obsessive person myself, I find such a laid-back approach quite difficult. But I comfort myself with three thoughts. First, as there is no way of generating a universally acceptable definition of the term it is best to learn to live with its ambiguity. Second, although we lack a definition of 'the spiritual' there is a defined body of writing, and accompanying critical scholarship, that has been referred to as spiritual autobiography in the past and is now increasingly referred to as spiritual life writing. In other words, there is an identifiable tradition to work with, heterogeneous though it may be. Last, and most importantly, to proceed to explore the challenges of spiritual life writing within a pre-defined set of terms would be very limiting. I hope rather to discover through reading and writing a deeper understanding of the sense the spiritual makes in this world.

I have divided Part 1 of this book into three chapters:

1 *Ancient Practice, New Purpose* explores the ways in which today's spiritual writing might draw upon the rich traditions of the past.

2 *Locating the Sacred* shows how contemporary spiritual writing can re-form traditional perspectives and embrace materiality, embodiment and its own literary status.

3 *Craft and Creativity* considers method in spiritual life writing and the particular challenge of naming spiritual experience. It concludes with some brief reflections on my own journeys in spiritual writing that have taken me so far from Eden.

I

Ancient Practice, New Purpose

Living in interesting times

This is a very creative period in which to explore the spiritual potential of writing about experience. A reflexive[1] turn in contemporary culture has generated a new respect for the knowledge that can be gained by turning curious attention to the intense vitality of everyday life. We are now more inclined to concede that our grasp of what is of utmost significance is as likely to be emotional and embodied as it is to be critical and rational. Instead of seeing spiritual understanding as always requiring distance and detachment we are also learning to value the wisdom that can come through deeply engaged practice. Furthermore, new paradigms and techniques are developing to facilitate personal reflection as well as the use of experience in academic research. In spiritual direction, contemplation, professional development, theological reflection and vocational formation people are, enthusiastically (or rather nervously), writing about their lives.

These are exciting times. But they are also confusing ones. Just at the point when it is now judged valid and fruitful to celebrate the revelatory significance of particular human experiences we are also facing some fundamental questions concerning the processes and products of personal reflection.

---

1 The sociologist Anthony Giddens (1991) argues that within postmodern culture people are called upon to construct an identity and self-narrative in an endeavour he describes as the 'reflexive project of the self'.

In some traditional paradigms an intense focus upon the self has been assumed to lead inevitably towards that inner dimension of the person called by certain traditions 'the spirit'.

> This spiritual core is the deepest centre of the person. It is here that the person is open to the transcendent dimension; it is here that the person experiences ultimate reality (Cousins *et al.*, cited in Taves 2003, p. 191).

In this model what is true and real lies within and constitutes the eternal essence of personhood. Other paradigms, that have been shaped by contemporary cultural theories,[2] would challenge this vision of a unified and interior selfhood and offer different models of encounters with transcendence that are complicated, fragmented and partial – and are as likely to occur in the flux and flow of life as through intense interiority.

As if this were not problematic enough, growing tensions exist in our understanding of the nature of autobiographical writing. Once it might have been assumed that if a writer endeavours with utmost seriousness to give an honest account of events they have experienced then their writing could be justifiably regarded as a factual account. Whether facticity has a place in spiritual narration is a question for later. We must first acknowledge the prior problem that taken-for-granted distinctions between fact and fiction that were once so useful in discussions concerning authenticity and truth now appear increasingly problematic. Modern literature certainly does not live in this divided kingdom, and philosophers such as Paul Ricoeur have taught us to appreciate how our experience is

---

2 Daniel Miller, for example, argues that we have an unwarranted respect for depth ontology: 'The assumption is the being we truly are is located deep inside ourselves and is in direct opposition to the surface. A clothes shopper is shallow because a philosopher or saint is deep . . . But these are all metaphors. Deep inside ourselves is blood and bile not philosophical certainty' (Miller 2010, p. 16).

never primal, but story-structured through and through (see, for example, Ricoeur 1991, p. 473).

Of course it is possible to carry on 'simply writing' and not pay much attention to these lively debates. However, to ignore them would be a shame. They are interesting. If we engage with them fully, we could find that creative paths open before us. But if emerging new territories in spiritual life writing are now appearing, in what ways do these relate to the traditions of the past? Returning to examine these will enable us to set our bearings and aid us in charting new explorations.

Establishing coherence

Spiritual autobiographies constitute one of the most ancient literary forms. Because of their long history and influential place in the development of Western culture they have decisively shaped modern autobiographical writing. And, more than this, many scholars believe they have also deeply influenced the way we understand human personhood and communicate what is most important about ourselves to others.

Many contemporary critical texts on autobiographical writing begin with the *Confessions* of Saint Augustine (Augustine 1963 [397–400]). Borrowing the structure of his narrative from the tales of quests, battles and heroes that were the popular cultural resources of his time (Staude 2005, p. 257), Augustine fashions a stirring narrative of exile and homecoming, struggles against dangerous forces, and the salvation of a hero who triumphs through submission. His genius is to meld familiar and well-understood themes into a new creation that is now distinctively Christian. The work resolutely affirms a self that can only find its own true being in relation to its Creator. In particular, Augustine's testimony to his conversion, and a new way of being in Christ, brings his self and his story into coherence. The wayward aspects of his experience are braided together into a form in which they all can be understood as significant and meaningful within God's providential purposes.

The process of transforming the muddle of experience into the coherence of faith provides an organizing basis for the many conversion narratives that have been constructed according to the pattern of *Confessions* over the centuries. While variously recording the journeys of saints and sinners, poets and mystics (Tredennick 2011), these stories share many common features as they present a journey from awakening to renewed life. Within them the author's conversion retrospectively confers order upon their experience, 'transforming what had been experienced at the time as discrete events into episodes in the process of conversion. Any apparent discontinuities . . . are thus retrospectively resolved into a continuous, coherent whole by that all-important endpoint, the converted, Christian self' (Tredennick 2011, p. 166). Although we glean many interesting insights into the particular circumstances and personalities of the authors of these narratives, we must do so by reading their works against the grain. The information the authors are seeking to convey is not about exciting encounters they have had en route to their spiritual destination. Their desire is rather to demonstrate the truth of the path they are presenting to their readers in order that others might also follow.

The expectations modern readers bring to autobiographical writing are thus confounded in much of the spiritual writing we inherit prior to the modern era. We are not being offered the unique life experience of a particular person, but instead gifted with a template of how a life can become meaningful as it finds its place in a much 'truer' redemptive story. In the spiritual writings of our forebears we thus often encounter what Bryan Rasmussen describes as 'generic selves' (Rasmussen 2010, p. 172) rather than modern individuals. This discrepancy between contemporary autobiographies and traditional spiritual narratives became very clear to me when I spent some time researching the final testimonies of Anabaptist martyrs. I was struck by the fact that the messages they painfully recorded for their loved ones and fellow believers were often remarkably uniform.³ Most followed very similar forms and said very similar things. Even as they faced death, the writer's chief hope was not to memorialize a particular self but to reinforce the pattern of a Christ-centred life.

As forms of reformed Christianity took root, spiritual self-examination gained in significance. No longer able to rely upon the mediating power of the Church to diagnose sin and assure forgiveness, it became more important for Protestant believers to attend carefully to personal intuitions of guilt and grace – and this could be a fearful process.⁴ Ordinary people became increasingly concerned to assess their spiritual health – and also to write about this frankly, and frequently at length! These narratives were often circulated within communities and sometimes published for the inspiration and edification of others. Commenting upon the proliferation of religious self-narratives, the historian Christopher Hill claims that from the late seventeenth century onwards we see the birth of an important new writing genre, 'Spiritual biographies of ordinary people' (Hill 1988, p. 64).

Diverse types of people were now taking pen to paper and recording their spiritual journeys, but we should not assume a new creative freedom automatically accompanied this democratization. Strong conventions still governed both the sentiments expressed and the manner of their expression. However, the very process of paying acute attention to the conflicts of the inner life *and writing about these things* certainly contributed to a growing cultural fascination with interiority. In a rapidly changing context in which fixed social roles were also being challenged, this interest contributed to the emerging individualism that was to characterize early industrial societies at the start of the modern era. In this new context, dramatically

---

3 At least in the form we inherit them. See, for example, van Bright (1938 [1660]).

4 Anxiety concerning salvation is widespread in many influential spiritual testimonies – such as John Bunyan's *Grace Abounding* (Bunyan 1907 [1666]).

different forms of 'spiritual' writing began to develop. This change can be illustrated with reference to the self-understanding of the romantic poets and thinkers whose work transformed the cultural and religious landscape from the late eighteenth century onwards.

Augustine and his followers had established their sense of coherence in the reconciliation of self with God's providential purposes. The Romantics, in a radical inversion of this pattern, saw the particular conditions of a human life as fashioning a distinct and unique individual whose highest purpose was to give form to that individuality through intense subjectivity and works of artistic or intellectual creation. Self-realization through self-expression became a substitute form of the spiritual quest – just as daunting and potentially perilous as previous forms had been. The same requirements to look inward for authentic knowledge and to construct a unifying thread joining apparently unconnected experiences remained. However, while some of the conventions of spiritual biography endured, their new employment was to describe the journey towards intense subjectivity and creative selfhood. This implied a rejection of social control and external authorities, including that of a controlling deity; although a fascination with the 'divine within' remained.

What is remarkable is that popular piety very quickly absorbed and thoroughly adapted to this transformed cultural understanding of human personhood. Because the inner life remained of huge importance in Romanticism and the self still possessed a 'sacred' aspect, the language and idioms of the movement were soon employed devotionally by quite orthodox believers. They seemed to marry well with images and symbols already important to them: the transformed heart, the renewed mind, the indwelling spirit and the self-shaking of sublime encounters (see Santmire and Cobb 2006). In many evangelical households, including those of my own forebears, the works of Romantic poets and thinkers sat happily alongside collections of devotional writings – and were equally valued for the spiritual sustenance and inspiration they offered. I inherited many of these 'ancestral' books and still keep them ranked alongside each other in my study. However, they are not only the poignant reminders of an age that has now passed. The self-interrogating ethos of the Reformation, the affective gestures of evangelical religion, and the questing, heroic self of Romantic thinking can all still be identified within contemporary spiritual writing.[5] We encounter their traces in the language of 'self-actualization', 'being true to myself', 'finding the real me' – all of which have more recognizably theological counterparts in popular discourses of conversion. This is now frequently presented as the restoration of an authentic self, 'the person God wants me to be'. Their echoes also sound in the frequently proclaimed 'I am not religious but I am spiritual', itself a Romantic assertion of the possibility of an unmediated and unregulated knowledge of the sacred that is associated with a rejection of institutions and dogmatic forms (see Heelas 2008).

Allowing for chaos

The narrative I produced above is a hugely condensed, but nevertheless serious and informed, attempt to chart the development of forms of spiritual autobiography from the early Christian period to the present day. Drawing upon the work of historians, sociologists and literary critics, I have constructed a coherent narrative that bundles up the wayward and diverse events of history into some kind of intelligible story. We need such stories to make sense of things and help us understand how we came to be the people we are.

However, they are always, in a manner of speaking, fictions.

We owe a great deal to the unsettling thinkers whose work dominated the last years of the twentieth century and who taught us to exercise a hermeneutics of suspicion when it comes

---

[5] No doubt their resilience is related to their usefulness within a modern Western capitalist context which also valorises a detached, heroic, seeking and choosing understanding of individual personhood.

to engaging with stories such as the one I presented above. Among these, Jacques Derrida, the prophet of deconstruction, encouraged us to ask, 'what story does an author seek to "untell", erase or write over when an authoritative narrative is presented?' (Derrida 1997). Michel Foucault reminded us that apparently neutral accounts of historical developments are discourses formed by the mechanisms of social power (Foucault 2002). Feminist thinkers, following on from Simone de Beauvoir (de Beauvoir 1972), have reminded us that women's perspectives have always been marginalized, forgotten and silenced in our re-tellings of the past.

It is important to bear in mind the challenges of these thinkers when approaching spiritual life writing because it is a very 'unstable' (or we might say gloriously peculiar) body of writing. It might seem strange to use the word unstable in reference to the traditions associated with Augustine's magisterial work. However, his writing deconstructs itself before our eyes as its author struggles to overwrite his own agency and present God as the author of his life and, in some sense therefore, also the author of his text. Larry Sissons describes the traditions of spiritual life writing that follow Augustine as inevitably split and skewed; they are 'eccentric', because there is a literal off-centring that 'unsettles notions of individual, independent and freely determined authorship' (Sissons 1998, p. 98). Linda Anderson goes further and argues that Augustine can be credited with establishing the autobiographical tradition with its authoritative narrative 'I'. Yet, at the same time, he undermines this project through his creaturely acknowledgement of the illusory nature of the independent and singular self; coherence and chaos struggle together in his writing (Anderson 2004, p. 27).

We can see similar tensions in the spiritual narratives of the post-Reformation period. Their authors strive to present the self redeemed, transformed by grace and resting in the Saviour's bosom. Yet the works are riven by the anxieties of abandonment, dissolution and the fear of fundamental error. 'Perhaps I know not either myself or my God' is the haunting subtext of many apparently confident pietist and evangelical texts. We might recognize a similar disturbing instability in the Romantic narratives of the creative self. It requires the creative work to establish the artistic self (as in, for example, Wordsworth's *The Prelude* (1969 [1850]), a long poem in which he explores the development of his sense of poetic vocation). However, the project undermines its own goals, rendering the self a product of the imaginative work. An internal unravelling undermines the coherence of the romantic self/text.

I do not think we should be either surprised or disturbed by the evident instability of these various forms of spiritual life writing. They have emerged from attempts to represent the self – but it is always the self as refracted through the presence of a sublime 'other'. They are thus necessarily provisional, contingent and marked by alterity. However, it is not only factors intrinsic to spiritual writing that unsettle the coherence of the texts. There are also more mundane issues to consider. Spiritual life writing cannot be abstracted from the social conditions in which it is produced; culture, context, class, race and gender mark this writing and bring their own creative disorder to the genre. Joanna Brooks offers persuasive illustrations of the ways in which social location impacts upon the work of two black spiritual life writers who offer us much more fragmented, 'worldly, discontinuous – yet intimate' (Brooks 2013, p. 951) accounts of the spiritual life.

In her discussion of the *Interesting Narrative of Olaudah Equiano* (Equiano 2004 [1789]), Brooks engages with the autobiographical reflections of an 'African who traces his roots to the Jews and a baptized Anglican who finds his most profound spiritual experiences in Methodism and yet continues . . . a "church man"' (Brooks 2013, p. 950). Equiano is not only a wanderer in religious terms: his life is subject to the ongoing social and existential crises that marked black Atlantic life in the eighteenth century. He records the intense brutalities of slavery, personal struggles, spiritual attachments and abandonments as well as literal and metaphorical departures from home. Brooks claims the narrative 'breaks from the conventions of eighteenth-century spiritual autobiographies' (Brooks 2013, p. 949), because it does not contrive to present the conventional forms of redeemed identity to the world. His writings offer penetrating insights into a spirituality that is punctuated by breaks, doubts, transitions and fallings away. Yet this provisional, open-ended account is deeply engaging to the contemporary reader in a way that ordered and conventional spiritual narratives are not. We feel invited to participate in the informal, everyday spirituality of the story as if at a soul feast where we 'join in the breaking of the bread and the passing round of mugs of water' (Brooks 2013, p. 950).

Brooks offers another challenging case study as she examines the work of the African American writer James Baldwin. Baldwin is celebrated for his rich, passionate accounts of black church life that draw heavily upon his own participation in this vibrant tradition (see, for example, Baldwin's *Go Tell it on the Mountain*, 2001). He also has produced one of the classic texts of gay literature in *Giovanni's Room* (Baldwin 2007). Baldwin's sexual identity meant that he could/would not rest in the place of his religious formation. 'What space could Baldwin claim . . . as a gay black Pentecostal? Where within these traditions might he be fully present before God and his fellow believers' (Brooks 2010, p. 445)? Yet he claimed through essays and fiction, *through writing*, a title to dwellings otherwise 'uninhabitable' for him. Through it all he had the wisdom and the grace to declare:

> Human history reverberates with violent upheaval, uprooting and departure, hello and good-bye. Yet I am not sure anyone ever leaves home . . . every life moves full circle towards revelation (Baldwin, cited in Brooks 2010, p. 448).

As Brooks argues, testimonies to nomadic spiritual identities such as that of Baldwin (he can neither dwell within or outside his tradition) might inspire a greater understanding of contemporary borderland spiritualities.

ANCIENT PRACTICE, NEW PURPOSE

Equiano and Baldwin are read by Brooks as representatives of the many others who could not easily inhabit the conventional structures of spiritual narration and have thus been moved to inscribe new paths which we might fruitfully trace today. Among these, numerous women have felt similarly 'at home and excluded' within the dominant traditions of spiritual autobiographies and have also contributed to generation of diversity within the genre (Magro 2004). In her engaging study of women's life writing in the period between 1760 and 1840, Amy Culley (Culley 2014) offers an account of the spiritual writings of early Methodist women. What is striking to her is that many of the accounts she studies are not works of self-narration but rather testimonies to relational selves. Many lives are intertwined within the texts. Spiritual journeys are shared. The works move between autobiography and biography as the focus changes between the self and the beloved others (often other women) who make up the community. Furthermore, the accounts lack the formality (pomposity?) and structural coherence of many male-authored works. Often they are affective, informal, homely, composite texts incorporating extracts from letters, obituaries and journal entries. These works 'complicate our understanding of religious self-narration', writes Culley (Culley 2014, p. 14) and encourage us to recover neglected aspects of the tradition:

> [Autobiography is] traditionally associated with the rise of individualism and it is understood as a genre that developed out of the puritan conversion narrative and in its emphasis on rigorous self-examination, individual experience and personal testimony. However, relationships are central to these women's self-representations, as they . . . demonstrate the interdependence of self and other and write a shared history. Approaching spiritual autobiography as an individualist mode has worked to obscure the collaborations that often underpin these works (Culley 2014, p. 19).

An irregular inheritance

Alasdair MacIntyre famously described a tradition as 'an argument extended through time' (MacIntyre 1988, p. 12). We might see the traditions of spiritual life writing as, if not an argument, certainly a heated conversation incorporating many twists, turns and changes in emphasis. Certain voices have been dominant but others have introduced divergent perspectives that have the potential to change our writing practice as it moves forward into the future. If, as I believe, our current cultural context demands from us new forms of spiritual writing, then the resources required for renewal may be found in deeply rooted elements of the tradition that have radical potential.

How we understand the challenges of our own time is clearly important here. It will determine which resources from the past we seek out and look to redeploy. Two diverging assessments of the way we live now struggle together within contemporary thinking – and they would lead us to take rather different approaches to our inherited tradition.

The first approach tells a story of loss: loss of faith in *all* traditional structures of belief (Lyotard 1984) and loss of hope in radical social change (Baudrillard 1994).

These 'losses' can be linked to the dominance of a capitalist system that threatens the environment and offers only illusory material compensations for the destruction of spiritual and human goods. This is a rather bleak analysis – but there is enough we recognize within it to cause us to acknowledge its challenge. It generates images of the spiritual journey today as a quest for new forms of coherence taking place in an alien land; a wasted place without landmarks and signposts. Indeed David Leigh, in his important work on spiritual life writing, characterizes the contemporary spiritual autobiographer as 'an alienated seeker . . . struggling with the lack of a stable sense of self . . . [and] a paralyzing environment' (Leigh 2000, p. 38).

ANCIENT PRACTICE, NEW PURPOSE

There is certainly cause to mourn the losses that modernity[6] has inflicted upon us and to fear for the future of our delicate planet with its delicate human cultures. However, even those who are making a twilight search for ways of believing that might still hold the world together may not wish to see old forms of coherence re-established. The artfully 'closed' spiritual stories of the past will not satisfy today's stubborn seekers in the half-light. The traditions of Augustine, Bunyan, Dante, Milton and others will continue to inspire through their audacity to articulate providential love among circumstances of personal and political upheaval. However, it is because their 'eccentric' and vulnerable faith is articulated from within, not beyond, the maelstrom of human experience that these traditions continue to offer sustenance today.

A second trajectory in contemporary thought offers a more positive view of our current situation. In this, attention is drawn to the gifts that accompany our griefs. It celebrates a new sense of wonder that is being generated out of our recognition that we belong within the natural and material orders as embodied creatures (Bennett 2010). It affirms the pragmatic improvisations taking place in politics and ethics (Haraway 1991). It draws attention to the intricate networks in which we are embedded and challenges all notions of separate and discrete, heroic selfhood (Latour 2005). It reminds us that we live in an age in which we can affirm diversity and in which women can confidently articulate their perspectives on matters holy and profane; although it also warns of restricted access to these freedoms – and their fragility. While no one could deny the immense challenges of inequality and environmental damage, this approach points also to the resilient resistance these conditions are generating. In this perspective we do not wander

---

6 Debates about whether to describe our age as modernity, late modernity or postmodernity continue – although with less vigour than in the past. I do not hold that there is no decisive break between eras and am happy to use all of these terms as seems most appropriate.

like lost children upon a dark plain but dwell in a place of light and shadows. Thus, in contrast to Leigh, we could describe the spiritual writer, according to this second mode of thinking, as an adaptive and pragmatic borrower from traditions, an embodied and relational self, a creative protester – both resisting and remaking – in an ambiguous but enchanted environment.

For there are also good reasons to celebrate modernity's gifts to us. Among the greatest of these may be the loss of innocent faith. An embodied and relational self does not seek to lift itself beyond this messy, complicated world, but rather seeks to adore the sacred within its blemished beauty. From the traditions of spiritual life writing 'adaptive borrowers' will pick out for reuse spiritual insights formed on the margins that may be fragmented, wayward, heterodox and contrary – but that are also evocative, inspiring and imaginative. Pragmatic and unprincipled as they may be, they will not reject the authoritative traditions of the genre. How lovely, how haunting and how compelling are its attempts to respond to a challenge from beyond the self that brings the self to chaos as it is artfully reborn.

Elements from all these precious sources can surely also be incorporated into new modes of spiritual writing.

2

Locating the Sacred

Worldly and bodily?

I struggle with Augustine, but in my heart I also love him. How could I not when he gave us words like these?

> Late have I loved Thee, O Beauty so ancient and so new; late have I loved Thee! For behold Thou wert within me, and I outside; and I sought Thee outside and in my unloveliness fell upon those lovely things that Thou hast made. Thou wert with me and I was not with Thee. I was kept from Thee by those things, and yet had they not been in Thee, they would not have been at all. Thou didst call and cry to me and break open my deafness: and Thou didst send forth Thy beams and shine upon me and chase away my blindness: Thou didst breathe fragrance upon me, and I drew in my breath and do now pant for Thee: I tasted Thee, and now hunger and thirst for Thee: Thou didst touch me, and I have burned for Thy peace (*Confessions* 10.27).

The words express the anguish of a desire for God that is somehow all bound up with a love of beautiful, created things that both do and don't draw us closer to their creator. The words tug and wrestle with one another to articulate spiritual yearnings for something that surpasses earthly desire. Yet we also sense that they are generated out of the passions of someone who has been moved in the flesh by the glories of this world.

Although in the past the spiritual has been understood oppositionally as *not*-worldly, *not*-bodily, reading passages such as this allows us to witness the contrary forces that have always been at work in spiritual writing. Throughout the centuries wild longings have been allowed, and even approved, within the genre. This is because their passion appears contained within the frame of the narrative itself and the wider interpretative tradition. The Spirit overwhelms the flesh and transposes its passions on to higher objects – as Augustine (rather unconvincingly) maintains. But in contemporary forms of spiritual life writing we are not able to sublimate our desires in this way. We have to deal with the world – spiritually. We have to touch the body. The old dualisms, which lifted the reader safely above the material order, no longer support our thinking.

We have to find ways to acknowledge this transformed outlook within our contemporary work. However, once again we can borrow from and re-form those spiritual traditions that have long celebrated the world we live in and the bodies we are. To be sure these rarely directly challenge philosophical distinctions between the material and the spiritual, but rather stress their interrelationship and take an affirmative view of creaturely existence as a spiritual path. I have been particularly influenced by the earthy common sense and intense joy to be found within the English mystical tradition, and in particular the works of the seventeenth-century writer Thomas Traherne:

> Your Enjoyment of the World is never right, till you so Esteem it, that evry thing in it, is more your Treasure, than a King's Exchequer full of Gold and Silver . . . Can you take too much Joy in your fathers Works? He is Himself in evry Thing. Som Things are little on the outside and Rough and Common – but I remember the Time, when the Dust of the Streets were as precious as Gold to my Infant Eys (Traherne 1966, p. 176).

In the idiosyncratic lineage of English mysticism we also have William Blake. The bundle of sources and influences he drew upon in the creation of his (eccentric) theological systems could not be described as materialist in any modern sense, but they resound with love for the mystical the substance of this world

> To see a World in a Grain of Sand
> And a Heaven in a Wild Flower (Blake 1979a, p. 209).

just as much as they thunder against sexual repression, economic oppression, and the exploitative abuse of human bodies:

> How the Chimney-sweepers cry
> Every blackning Church appalls,
> And the hapless Soldier's sigh,
> Runs in blood down Palace walls (1979b, p. 53).

Alongside mystical traditions such as these we can place the deeply incarnational forms of theological understanding that have formed one of the strongest, brightest threads in Western Christianity. Saint Francis is often taken as a representative figure for this tradition. In his poetry, theological vision and dramatic actions (such as living among lepers and bringing donkeys into church), we find a living symbolics of wonder – that is the complementary aspect of his espousal of poverty. As the Franciscan tradition developed, reflections upon the presence of God manifest in the selfness of all creatures flowered in theology. Ilia Delio describes the radical materiality inherent in the work of those shaping this dynamic thinking:

> For Scotus and for Bonaventure, the universe is the external embodiment of the inner Word of God . . . Bonaventure writes that in his transfiguration Christ shares existence with all things: with the stones he shares existence, with the plants he shares life, with animals he shares sensation . . . 'In his human nature,' he stated, 'Christ embraces something of every creature in himself' (Delio 2003, p. 19).

Franciscan influences are to be found embedded in the spirituality of the Jesuit tradition – Ignatius himself was deeply influenced by Franciscan writing. Jesuits have practised and supported others in disciplined efforts to discern the will of God for the believer in every aspect of life. Following Ignatius they have also sought to imagine with every embodied sense the revelation of God as if it were taking place directly before them in this moment.[1] Within this religious community has thus developed an acute attentiveness to the world as a theatre of grace.[2] This has been instantiated in many forms, including the espousal of liberation theologies in the case of the six Jesuit martyrs of El Salvador[3] and the contemporary orientation of the Jesuits towards the service of the poor. I have found it delightfully expressed in the work of Michel de Certeau, a radical and unconventional Jesuit of very uncertain orthodoxy who pursued his own spiritual journey among the intellectual giants of France during the radical 1960s and 1970s.

De Certeau was fascinated and inspired by the everyday practices through which people created neighbourhoods, cooked meals, cradled babies and enjoyed conviviality. Trained in modes of spiritual attentiveness by modern Jesuit thinkers, he perceived these commonplace actions as spiritual achievements. In the face of the global economic systems that seek to contain human creative powers he marvelled that we resist 'with sweet obstinacy' (de Certeau *et al.* 1998, p. 213) through such ordinary gestures as these. When we turn a discerning eye to the everyday world, he argues, we can observe how wrong it is to dismiss people as passive consumers of the goods the system provides (see Walton 2014, pp. 180–3). Rather, they are

---

1 Ignatius advised spiritual seekers 'to smell and to taste with the senses of smell and taste the infinite gentleness and sweetness of the divinity . . . to touch with the sense of touch – as, for instance, to embrace and kiss' the places made holy by the divine presence 'always taking care to draw profit from this' (see Ivens 1998, pp. 96–8).

2 This is the tradition at its perceptive best.

3 They were murdered alongside their housekeeper and her daughter in 1989.

'unrecognized producers, poets of their own acts, silent discoverers of their own paths in the jungle of functional rationality' (de Certeau, 1984, p. xviii).

In the work of thinkers like de Certeau we receive a clear challenge to create forms of spiritual writing that are located in the common experiences of everyday life. However, spiritual and religious writers often still prefer to represent our spiritual lives in terms that emphasize the importance of the natural order rather than our cultural life together. It remains easier for us to imagine an encounter with the divine when alone in a forest or high up on a mountain than it is in a busy city street or family kitchen. However, just as Scotus and Bonaventure taught us how to imagine the whole universe as the external embodiment of God, de Certeau encourages us to discern the sacred incarnate within the particular, the intimate and the domestic. It will require courageous experimentation to do so, for we strain against the limits that truly incarnational thinking represents. We still do not wish to name God in small and tiny things that are apparently of no account. And we still have problems with bodies.

But perhaps for different reasons than in times past.

Much recent research confirms how popular holistic thinking has now become and how people from many differing religious traditions, and none, now identify a fundamental coherence between body and spirit (see Heelas and Woodhead 2005; Heelas 2008). In many Western traditions we are moving away from a belief that human beings have bodies to an understanding that human beings are bodies. Embodiment is now frequently represented not in terms of temporal limits, but in terms of spiritual possibilities. We can affirm the spirituality of motherhood, of sexuality, of sport, of ageing, etc.

Our theological systems are still in the early days of engagement with a transformed understanding of embodiment that will fundamentally reshape our conceptual frameworks. Important challenges lie ahead, but these are not my chief concern here. In terms of life writing, G. Thomas Couser argues that the most significant development in the twentieth century was the new emphasis placed upon what it means be a particular kind of body (Couser 2007, p. 79). As spiritual writing responds to this development, I am anxious that alongside a celebration of embodiment we learn how to name the limits, griefs and tragedies of the flesh. At one time these could be understood and dealt with, *sub specie aeternitatis*,[4] as painful but provisional experiences – of significance chiefly in their capacity to deliver spiritual challenges. Now we need to acknowledge their profound impact upon us. My own deep awareness of embodiment was stamped upon me not by sensuous enjoyment, aesthetic intensity, feminist epistemology or sublime experiences in nature. It came through infertility. The grinding, everyday pain of being unable to conceive. Sonja Boon writes out of the very different experience of suffering permanent, painful disability through giving birth. Her words trouble the affirmative discourses of embodiment that have become common currency today:

> This body speaks. But it does not speak to the institution of motherhood. It is wary. It has been marked. It has been rejected. In its suffering it is a rejecting body. Rejecting maternity. Rejecting motherhood. Rejecting the mother. My body is restless. Rooting. Wandering. Searching. Buried in my flesh, a clinging desperation. A haunted body that seeks an audience. That wants to speak. A story that resists its telling even as it yearns for an audience.
>
> And in the silence, my body speaks. It speaks through its resistance. It cries out. Weeping. Grieving its maternity. Grieving its materiality (Boon 2012, p. 197).

She is able to declare, however, 'My grief, an open wound. My wound, the site of possibility, potential, wonder' (Boon 2012, p. 195) and to link together suffering and the birthing processes. These brave sentiments, it seems to me, need to find their space and acknowledgement in our spiritual writing.

---

4 From the perspective of the eternal.

Writing and witnessing

I remember, when I first began to preach from carefully handwritten scripts (I actually still preach from carefully handwritten scripts, but they contain more crossings out than previously), an elderly Church Steward came up and gently admonished me, 'Don't you know', he said, 'that the letter killeth but the Spirit givest life.' Felicity Nussbaum notes a similar mistrust of writing as something artificial and potentially at odds with the spiritual life in her exploration of evangelical spiritual autobiographies. To conform to piety the writing should ideally become transparent and erase its own presence, 'while spiritual self-reflection was sanctioned in spiritual self-writing, writerly self reflection was not' (Nussbaum 1989, p. 176). Commenting upon this aversion, Bryan Rasmussen notes the paradox that spiritual life writing often emerged out of 'a religious culture . . . that was, for various reasons, against writing' (Rasmussen 2010, p. 165).

An anxiety about writing is not confined to works of spiritual self-narration. Derrida has argued that it has its roots in the metaphysical systems that form Western culture (Derrida 2001). Writing is seen as secondary to speech: it cannot represent the full presence of lived encounters, it is mimetic, potentially inauthentic and generally untrustworthy. To become moderately reliable it has to be self-effacing and give a plain account of things in as factual a manner as possible. The problem is that the heights of spiritual experience, and indeed the depths of any experience, are not easily rendered in plain terms. We need images, metaphors and symbols to tentatively approach them. But once we use these we are, in a sense, constructing an obvious distance between the experience and its representation. We risk privileging the words above the event. This is a very difficult problem.

It has been most fiercely debated in relation to the literature of the Holocaust and it is through this debate we can begin to understand the very high stakes at play in contesting positions. There are many who would argue that once we start to make art out of intense human suffering on an unimaginable scale we are dishonouring the dead. To respect them we should present the facts with stark simplicity and leave the rest as silence. However, others would argue that unimaginable situations have to be imagined to become communicable and that manifesting intensity is the business of art.

Holocaust witnesses and writers themselves have been divided on this topic. Elie Wiesel has stated that, while a literature of testimony is required, the work of forming any kind of account of the Holocaust is a gesture against impossibility and only conceivable at all if the writer is not speaking *as a writer* but *as a witness* – someone who offers their own witness-testimony while intensely conscious of their inability to meet the requirements of this sacred duty. In contrast, Imre Kertész, another survivor of Auschwitz, argues that the 'concentration camp is imaginable only and exclusively as literature' (cited in Bachmann 2009, pp. 79–80), through the creative transformation accomplished through the work of writing. Some events will be omitted, others highlighted, narrators become characters, and authors impose a fictional frame on events. In other words, imagination must override experience in order to release it from the possession of those few who were actually present and who can offer account. Only through literature can lasting memorials be made.

In an article exploring the tensions between these two positions, Michael Bachmann emphasizes that literature 'follows different rules to those of reality' (Bachmann 2009, p. 87) and the 'rule' of literature is to turn experience into fiction. Of course, most spiritual life writers are not wrestling with traumatic events on the scale confronted by Wiesel and Kertész. However, they may well be witnesses to events that present a compelling need to be told – and also defy straightforward telling. These could be experiences of suffering or grace. Recording these might seem a nearly impossible but sacred duty. To confess them, the writer might find they must begin to learn the rules of fiction.

Fiction and lies

'Authentic things are original, real and pure. They are what they purport to be', writes Charles Lindholm (Lindholm 2013, p. 363). As discussed previously, within our culture the spiritual quest is frequently viewed as the search for an 'authentic' self as well as a truth to live by. No less than the spiritual autobiographers of previous centuries, we are suspicious of 'writerly' techniques that appear to diminish the simple purity of our seeking. Any suggestion that spiritual life writing is intrinsically a fictional process can appear to challenge the foundations of the genre.

But perhaps we need to look again at what we understand by fiction?

In Lucy Caldwell's novel *All the Beggars Riding* (2014), the principal character, Lara, feels her life is blighted by the lies, silences and absences of her parents. As an adult she is unable to make sense of what she has experienced until she starts to write about it. Even then she struggles with the gaps in her understanding until her creative writing tutor urges her to use fictional methods to tell her own story:

> You have this thing against fiction don't you Lara? You think because you are telling a true story only the exact and utter truth will do. It's like a moral imperative for you. But actually everything we write is a kind of story. We shape it, we structure it, decide where it begins and ends. You say that you are stumbling into blanks and holes – well what fiction can do is spin a net across them . . . People always talk about fiction as if it's an escape from the world, but it's not that, or not just that. It's an escape out of ourselves and into the world too (Caldwell 2014, p. 124).

By the end of the novel, Lara has found a way to live with her own experiences, because she has realized that the process of writing is part of her own quest. She learns there is a huge distinction to be made between 'knowing things and writing them down' and 'understanding things through writing':

> Writing isn't self-expression . . . It's the taking and shaping of things, carefully, again and again, until they make a sort of sense that not only you but others can understand and maybe benefit from. At the start of this narrative I'm obsessed with knowing. I've come to realize you can never know but you can understand (Caldwell 2014, p. 238).

I am particularly struck by two small phrases from these quotations. The first is 'everything we write is a kind of story'. Contemporary philosophers and theorists have expended a great deal of time and energy demonstrating that narrative gives us the structure we call identity, creates knowledge systems and traditions, and gives us the resilience we need to adapt and survive in changing circumstances. Everything we write has to be a kind of story or else it would be unintelligible. But not only everything we write; everything we say, do and believe has a narrative quality to it. Of course, narrative, with its structuring and shaping mechanisms, removes us far from unmediated experience, and in this sense it is not innocent, or pure, or authentic. But it is the art we need to survive.

The second phrase that stands out is 'Writing isn't self-expression'. This might seem an anti-intuitive statement in the context of an essay about life writing. However, it serves as a healthy reminder that there is a whole world lying between the self and the page. To make a crossing we leave most of our history and experience behind. Because it is not useful or too heavy to carry, we have to take others with us as characters in our story or as assumed readers, and we must use all our creative and imaginative powers to get to the other side.

A recognition that fictional techniques form an integral aspect of autobiographical writing is one reason why the terminology to describe this work has shifted in recent years. The phrase life writing is more open and capacious than autobiography – which is now commonly seen as a narrower term (Lee 2005;

Saunders 2010). Its use signals a recognition that autobiography, biography and autobiographical fictions are often all present in the one text. It also helps us to refer to that growing body of hybrid work that does not fit easily into any neat category but clearly refers in some way or another to lived lives. Spiritual autobiographies, in both their mundane and sacred aspects, have always been more than stories of the self, and the looseness of the term is particularly helpful in this context.

While life writing offers more space for creative construction than autobiography, it does not mean that there are no longer any ethical obligations for the life writer as they fashion accounts of lives. This point is made very strongly by Paul John Eakin who states that 'when life writers fail to tell the truth, they do more than violate a literary convention . . . they disobey a moral imperative' (Eakin 2004b, pp. 2–3). While Eakin is much more defensive of the boundaries between fact and fiction than I would be, I concur with him that there is a danger of breach of trust when writers present imagined events and people within their life writing. However, we have to live with this ambiguity. Most life writers have found ways to signal within their texts whether they are presenting a fictional life, offering an ironic 'anti-biography' that still sits credibly within the genre, or using fictional techniques to express their life experiences. Once again, I remind myself that in a situation of inevitable ambiguity it is not productive to get too worried about defending borders. Furthermore, I have found that the truth is not easy to write. I often get closest to it right at the end of a writing process when I have struggled for a long time with how to present a character, event or experience. It is hardly ever the case that something can be just set down on paper and appear as it was in life. Perhaps it is never the case.

3
Craft and Creativity

Shaping your story

A discussion of the 'fictive' nature of spiritual writing moves us helpfully into a consideration of the craft of writing.

Writing about the self presents many challenges! Perhaps the most difficult is that you have to become the author of your own life. To begin with this means that your scope is not unlimited and you might be quite doubtful about the stuff you have to work with. As Norma Tilden writes, we are forever trying to piece together the scraps of a sort of life:

> They arrive unboxed. Lacking attachments and instructions. Upon examination you may discover stubborn stains, shredded selvedge, missing fasteners. This story was not, as your mother used to say of garments she wanted you to wear, 'made for you'. Nor is it you make it yourself . . . [There] is always a negotiation between what life offers you to work with and what you want to say (Tilden 2004, p. 710).

Tilden's words remind us not only that our resources are limited, but when we are stitching things together from the ragbag of a life, there might be materials we don't want to use. It may be that these are not appropriate to wear in public – or that they do not belong to us but to someone else. As well as the ethical duties we owe to our readers in relation to truth telling, we also have obligations not to tell the truth sometimes; we have to leave things out. There is a duty of self-care. Some events are very painful, and although we might want to seek relief through writing, we could regret our disclosures later. Other stories might harm others were they to become public – and limiting the flow of information is becoming increasingly difficult to secure. So it is important to take moral control of your narrative as you decide what is to be written and what is best unsaid.[1]

Taking moral control might seem easier than taking control of the telling of the story itself. You have to decide what kind of narrator you will be. You could be the kind of distant, omniscient creator who keeps control of the story as it unfolds on a directed and certain path. Or you could place yourself in the midst of events as an explorer and fellow-traveller with your reader. Linked to this decision is whether you are seeking to resolve the spiritual questions you raise within the space of your story, or are you going to leave the narrative open-ended and in a sense unfinished, allowing that there may not be a way of gaining adequate closure of difficult issues?

These are existential questions, but they are also literary ones. They relate to *character* and *plot* – the essential elements of narrative. They remind us that we are working within the conventions that structure all story-telling. And just as it is helpful to be aware of these conventions, it is also useful to be aware of techniques that can help us to shape good practice. In an earlier book, I set out a list of the 'tricks of the trade' that creative writing teachers urge upon their students. These are worth repeating here as a checklist to guide you in the construction of your story:

- Show, don't tell. It is always more effective to invite the reader to 'see' a situation than explain it to them.
- Less is more. Cut away what is not needed. Excess is never helpful.

---

[1] Paul John Eakin (ed.), *The Ethics of Life Writing* (2004), offers a range of ethical responses to the dilemmas inherent in self-narration.

- Signpost your path. Allow the reader to find their own way through a narrative, but provide them with the way-markers they need to do so.
- Do not fear the personal or the particular. These are your gift to your reader. They will have had intense experiences of their own that will enable them to enter into yours.
- Small is beautiful. It really is possible to see a world in a grain of sand – although it may take a little practice!
- Always revise, rewrite, revise. And then do so again.
- Rules are made to be broken. (Walton 2014, pp. xxvii–iii).

Useful as these techniques are, they might feel as if they are taking you a long way from the spiritual experiences that led you to wish to tell your story. It is worth balancing them with some very good advice from Douglas Hesse concerning what constitutes good writing from experience. He acknowledges that it requires craft and a careful shaping hand. But more is needed and he describes this as:

> [A]n insistent and celebratory sense that, while the author is writing about the world as it is and life as it happens, this truth is filtered through a consciousness *whose goal is to make us pay attention and to care* (Hesse 2009, p. 20, my italic).

Writerly techniques

As well as a consciousness that cares and shapes, good life writing requires 'language that surprises and delights' (Hesse 2009, p. 20). A one-dimensional account bereft of the use of image (a phrase that paints a picture) and symbol (an object that points to meanings beyond itself) would not awake the imagination. Its communicative power would be limited. This does not mean we have to use elaborate words or construct complicated phrases. Some of the most powerful images and symbols are ones that draw us deep into the stuff of everyday life rather than remove us from it. In the Bible, for example, the most powerful images are stark and archetypal: a tree, a woman weeping for her lost children, a rod striking a stone. The symbols also tend to be organic and fundamental: bread, wine, rock, water, light etc. They carry so many powerful associations because they are grounded in our experience, and their repeated use sustains their power. Proper nouns used carefully in imaginative writing are vivid and dynamic. They convey far more than the abstract phrases by which we often try, less successfully, to represent deep emotions.

Metaphors function rather differently from images and symbols in that they do not draw on the power of repeated association, but generate startling new understandings not previously realized. Their work is to draw dissimilar elements into new relationships and transform perception. Paul Ricoeur writes: 'Metaphor shatters not only the previous structures of our language but also the previous structures of what we call reality' (Ricoeur, in Valdés 1991, p. 85). The metaphors we create in spiritual life writing are likely to be those generated out of deep traditions brought into new conjunction with our lived performances of spirituality. For example, in my own early writing it was the experience of infertility that provided the strange new conjunctions of words I needed to write about God. Whatever is strong in your experience you should mine for its potential metaphors. They will be there.

As well as the common literary devices named above, there are also special ways of signifying moments of illumination within literature that are immensely helpful to the spiritual writer.

'Epiphany' is a term used within the Christian tradition to describe the self-revelation or showing of the divine. In poetics[2] it has a wider coinage and refers to those epiphanic moments in which a transfiguration of ordinary reality occurs, leading to

---

2 Poetics, as used here, refers to the conventions used by creative writers to construct their texts. These include image, symbol, metaphor, plot, characterization and other literary devices such as epiphanies.

personal change, a transformed understanding of the world, or simply heightened perception. Interestingly, in its use of epiphanies, Western literature is drawing upon the traditions of spiritual autobiography. Augustine's narrative employs epiphanic encounters, accounts of moments of intense significance such as when he hears a child's voice calling to him in the garden, to move its narrator towards his conversion. The process of using illuminative moments to show personal development is repeated and developed in the works known as *Bildungsroman*: a genre commonly held to have developed from Goethe's *Wilhelm Meister's Apprenticeship* (1989 [1795]). Sharon Kim describes this narrative tradition as:

> [A] genre that shapes its narrative structure around a character's education or growth . . . that often takes shape around an epiphany. Like stars in constellations, moments of sudden insight form structural nodes for the character, its identity and its increasing understanding of the world (Kim 2006, p. 155).

She goes on to describe how this tradition takes a variety of forms in twentieth-century writing. Edith Wharton, for example, used religious symbols and language to describe epiphanic moments as flashes of light irradiating a moment and forming a character. While Wharton is close to the traditions of spiritual writing and presents epiphanies as moral awakenings, James Joyce is more concerned to portray them as vital moments of uncovering in which the mind comprehends an object, an ordinary thing, 'its soul, its whatness, leaps to us from the vestment of its appearance' (Joyce, cited in Kim 2006, p. 151). In Joyce's later works this epiphanic shock is provoked not by an external object, but by a startling and compelling conjunction of words – that may defy normal sense but possess world-piercing power.

Clearly, a contemporary spiritual writer could usefully construct a narrative in the manner of Augustine, Goethe or Wharton as a series of epiphanic moments in which insight occurs leading to personal/moral development. This is an interesting and fruitful writing process. However, it is important not to dismiss the more literary insights of the a/religious Joyce. They take us into the mundane world of things, concrete and material objects, which are seen in a new frame as possessing their own revelatory 'whatness'. He also reminds us that words have power. As Deleuze writes, 'a spark can flash and break out of language itself, to make us see and think what was lying in the shadow around the words, things we were hardly aware existed' (Deleuze 1995, p. 41).

The use of the sublime in literature is also a common means to present a turning point in spiritual perception – usually of a rather dramatic kind. Although its origins lie in antiquity, the sublime became an important concept in the Enlightenment when philosophers were seeking to understand the relation between the mind, the senses and the world. Classically a moment of sublime recognition is the inner state occasioned by sensory encounters provoking feelings of awe, terror and finitude. This famous passage from Kant describes how in the face of natural forces the imagination falters:

> bold overhanging, as it were, threatening rocks, thunderclouds piling up in the sky . . . volcanoes with all their destructive power . . . the high waterfall of a mighty river, and so on. Compared to the might of these our ability to resist becomes a significant trifle (Kant, cited in Shaw 2006, pp. 82–3).

Kant is describing a mental state that in its registering of awe generates awareness that humans possess 'capacities that transcend the limitations of our own phenomenal existence' (Shaw 2006, p. 83). For him, it is not a religious experience per se. However, such experiences have frequently been used to describe a spiritual turning point in both fiction and life writing. Once again, they are commonly associated with the natural world – but need not be. Much has been written about the 'technological sublime' (see, for example, Nye 1996), an awe felt at the mastery of machines, the power of weaponry, the intricate patterns of circuits etc. It is also a concept that women writers have used to refer to the overwhelming and compelling nature of domestic life in which a person can feel reduced to nothingness or inspired to marvel at their place in the immensity of the procreative process (see, for example, Smart 1991 [1978], pp. 87–8).

It is worth pointing out that sublime encounters (of all kinds) are exhausting to experience and to read about! In a beautiful article containing advice to a young writer, Tarn Wilson quotes Annie Dillard's reflections on her sublime experience during an eclipse: 'Enough is enough. One turns from glory with a sigh of relief. From the depths of mystery, and even from the heights of splendor, we . . . hurry for the latitudes of home' (Wilson 2012, p. 150). So, Wilson adds, 'the most pleasing pieces of autobiographical writing make enough use of familiar narrative structure that the reader feels comfortable, but then, in some way explode . . . these forms' (Wilson 2012, p. 156). This is very good counsel. We need home comforts to balance out explosive bliss.

Writing the divine

'I realized that current forms of personal writing, shaped as they have been by the values of the academy, militate against writing about religion', writes Anne Ruggles Gere (in Brandt et al. 2001, p. 47). She recounts her personal self-censorship as a life writer and the difficulties she encountered in finding a language with the subtlety and flexibility of, for example, queer theory, to provide an intellectually credible and suitably evocative way of articulating the significance of her religious explorations in anything but the crudest and most conventional of terms.

This is undoubtedly a problem for the spiritual life writer who hopes their work will not be automatically dismissed as naively credulous, exotic or relevant only to those who share their particular convictions. However, it joins with a larger problem. The ancient symbolics of religion are marked by the contexts out of which they developed. Dominant motifs continue to be gendered, hierarchical and exclusive. Within the Christian tradition, Gordon Kaufman is well known for his efforts (Kaufman 1993 and 1995) to inspire other theologians to generate ethically acceptable God language that will undermine the social conservatism of the symbolism we currently routinely employ. He believes 'the symbol "God"' has been used to sustain a cosmic hierarchical pattern which sustains 'similar hierarchical patterns in human affairs; those who are male/white/wealthy/powerful determine the order to which those who are female/black/poor/weak must submit' (Kaufman 1993, p. 106).

Kaufman sees the work of reimagining God language as a necessary part of a political journey towards a more just and ecologically sustainable future (Kaufman 1993, p. 113). Many feminist theologians have shared this view and attempted to generate radically different ways of imaging God in their writing (see McFague 1993; Althaus-Reid 2000).[3] They have been particularly concerned to employ metaphoric language that celebrates the divine in female form, gestures against a disembodied and disengaged divinity and presents a challenge to earth-abusing political systems.

I have immense sympathy with these efforts and find they challenge me to creativity – both as a writer as well as a believer.[4] However, they are not without their problems. Old religious systems contain depth and wisdom as well as

---

3 For more detailed discussions of the creative use of language in theological thinking, see Walton 2007.

4 Incidentally the questions raised here are ones that have been debated for many years by writers and artists. How to create art that inspires faith in a 'secular' context in which the symbolics of religion are problematic remains a vexed topic (see, for example, Pell 1998).

difficulties. Furthermore, attempts to generate religious systems that are pure and free of the taint of the past seem to me to risk participating in a quest for innocence that generates as many problems as it resolves. Maybe it is important to acknowledge that all religious systems (including recently invented ones) are inherently dangerous? Having done so, we may certainly seek new and fresh ways of speaking about God – but also to try and 'turn' the symbols we inherit so that they begin to signify differently. As I have tried to show in the book thus far, radical insights can be discovered when the tradition is examined from a new angle.

Our creative efforts will not resolve the many problems associated with religious writing today. However, I am inspired to think that spiritual life writers have a particularly important role to play in contemporary efforts to reimagine the divine. This is because the religious language they use is not employed to substantiate metaphysical systems or doctrinal assertions – it is employed in order to explore what happens when people 'perform' their religious identities in everyday life. In relation to 'performativity', Judith Butler (Butler 1999) has argued that when people try to act out identities according to dominant social and cultural scripts (such as gender, ethnicity and, we could add, religion) they are not actually able to do so; we cannot embody the ideal type of 'woman', 'Scottish person' or 'Christian' that the social scripts mandate. We often thus make – small but nevertheless significant – adaptations to the parts we play which have the cumulative effect of producing change. In relation to spiritual life writing, Joanna Brooks argues that when engaging with this work we discover not the unchanging coherence of a tradition but rather the improvised performance of spiritual lives. These works contain 'fractal paths of revelatory discontinuities and creative heterodoxies' (Brooks 2010, p. 449) plotted within the life narratives. Through their creative 'failures' to conform, these living human documents constitute 'the very texture of contemporary faith' (Brooks 2010, p. 449).

CRAFT AND CREATIVITY

Writing a long way from Eden

It is not easy to write about the principles and practice of spiritual life writing as Part 1 of a book in which Part 2 consists of your own life writing. Throughout the process I have been asking myself how much my own work confirms or contradicts the messages I am trying to convey! All the more reason to keep this concluding section very brief. However, I do want to signal towards some of the specific things I have learnt about this craft over the years.

When I begin a new supervision journey with a doctoral student, I find that for the first few months the most frequent question they bring to our conversations is 'Am I allowed?' This question combines a host of anxieties. Am I allowed to write differently? Am I allowed to be interdisciplinary? Am I allowed to put my own voice in the research? Am I allowed to wander around and play a while, before I try and put my thoughts in order? My answer to all these questions is always YES. I would like to frame my concluding thoughts in a similarly permissive fashion.

In spiritual life writing you ARE allowed:

- To stray beyond realism. To place elements in your work that are parabolic, mythical or simply playful. You are presenting your experiences of the heights and depths of life – not a report to a municipal sub-committee on accounts.
- To use heightened language and every 'constructed' technique of poetics to enliven your text. Beautiful words are divine.
- Not to move from A to B by the most direct route. In fact, you might never get to B at all. The plot does not need to be linear and you are not mandated to undertake a one-way journey – backwards and forwards is fine.
- Not to have a happy ending. Or any ending at all (see above).
- To speak about God in all sorts of ways – and leave God out for whole chunks of the time (see the Bible for examples here).

- To love tradition and yet to struggle against it.
- To employ fiction to tell the truth – however, don't use real events to tell lies.
- To be honest about enduring griefs and the wounds of the body. And to be angry too.
- To balance the sublime with the mundane.
- To mention sex (but see above).

Is there any link between all these points? Yes. They are about writing that is not innocent; that has lost all nostalgia for the pure representations of pure forms. A writing that lives spiritually in this world – while still yearning in its travails. A writing that is at last acknowledging where its heart should lie and is learning to 'love the country of the here below' (Weil 2009, p. 66).

Bibliography

Althaus-Reid, Marcella, 2000, *Indecent Theology: Theological Perversions in Sex, Gender and Politics*, London: Routledge.
Anderson, Linda, 2004, *Autobiography*, London and New York: Routledge.
Augustine, 1963, *The Confessions of St Augustine*, trans. F. J. Sheed, London: Sheed & Ward.
Bachmann, Michael, 2009, 'Life, Writing, and Problems of Genre in Elie Wiesel and Imre Kertész', *Rocky Mountain Review*, 6.3, pp. 79–88.
Baldwin, James, 2001, *Go Tell it on the Mountain*, London: Penguin Classics.
Baldwin, James, 2007, *Giovanni's Room*, London: Penguin Classics.
Baudrillard, Jean, 1994, *Simulacra and Simulation*, Ann Arbor: University of Michigan Press.
Bennett, Jane, 2010, *Vibrant Matter: A Political Ecology of Things*, Durham, NC: Duke University Press.
Blake, William, 1979a [1803], 'Auguries of Innocence', in Mary Lynn Johnson and John E. Grant (eds), *Blake's Poetry and Designs*, New York: W. W. Norton, pp. 209–12.
Blake, William, 1979b [1794], 'London', in Mary Lynn Johnson and John E. Grant (eds), *Blake's Poetry and Designs*, New York: W. W. Norton, p. 53.
Boon, Sonja, 2012, 'Autobiography by Numbers; or, Embodying Maternal Grief', *Life Writing*, 9.2, pp. 191–202.
Brandt, Deborah *et al.*, 2001, 'The Politics of the Personal: Storying Our Lives Against the Grain', *College English*, 64.1, pp. 41–62.
Brooks, Joanna, 2010, 'From Edwards to Baldwin: Heterodoxy and New Narratives of American Literary History', *American Literary History*, 22.2, pp. 439–53.
Brooks, Joanna, 2013, 'Soul Matters', *PMLA*, 128.4, pp. 947–52.
Bunyan, John, 1907 [1678], *Grace Abounding and the Pilgrim's Progress*, Cambridge: Cambridge University Press.

Butler, Judith, 1999, *Gender Trouble: Feminism and the Subversion of Identity*, London: Routledge.
Caldwell, Lucy, 2014, *All the Beggars Riding*, London: Faber and Faber.
Couser, G. Thomas, 2007, 'Undoing Hardship: Life Writing and Disability Law', *Narrative*, 15.1, pp. 71–84.
Culley, Amy, 2014, *British Women's Life Writing 1760–1840: Friendship, Community, and Collaboration*, Basingstoke: Macmillan.
de Beauvoir, Simone, 1972 [1949], *The Second Sex*, trans. H. M. Parshley, London: Pan Books.
de Certeau, Michel, 1984, *The Practice of Everyday Life*, trans. Steven Rendall, Berkeley: University of California Press.
de Certeau, Michel, et al., 1998, *The Practice of Everyday Life, vol. 2: Living and Cooking*, Minneapolis: University of Minnesota Press.
Deleuze, Gilles, 1995, *Negotiations 1972–90*, trans. Martin Joughin, New York: Columbia University Press.
Delio, Ilia, 2003, 'Revisiting the Franciscan Doctrine of Christ', *Theological Studies*, 64, pp. 3–23.
Derrida, Jacques, 1997, *Of Grammatology*, trans. Gayatri Spivak, London: Johns Hopkins University Press.
Derrida, Jacques, 2001, *Writing and Difference*, trans. Alan Bass, London: Routledge.
Eakin, Paul John (ed.), 2004a, *The Ethics of Life Writing*, Ithaca and London: Cornell University Press.
Eakin, Paul John, 2004b, 'Mapping the Ethics of Life Writing', in Paul John Eakin (ed.), *The Ethics of Life Writing*, Ithaca and London: Cornell University Press, pp. 1–16.
Equiano, Olaudah, 2004 [1789], *The Interesting Narrative of the Life of Olaudah Equiano, or Gustavus Vassa, the African*, New York: The Modern Library.
Foucault, Michel, 2002, *Archaeology of Knowledge*, trans. A. M. Sheridan Smith, London: Routledge.
Giddens, Anthony, 1991, *Modernity and Self Identity: Self and Society in the Late Modern Age*, Cambridge: Polity Press.
Goethe, Johann Wolfgang von, 1989, *Wilhelm Meister's Apprenticeship*, ed. and trans. Eric A. Blackall, New York: Suhrkamp Publishers.
Haraway, Donna, 1991, *Simians, Cyborgs and Women: The Reinvention of Nature*, London: Free Association Books.
Heelas, Paul, 2008, *Spiritualities of Life: New Age Romanticism and Consumptive Capitalism*, Oxford: Blackwell Publishing.
Heelas, Paul, and Woodhead, Linda, 2005, *The Spiritual Revolution: Why Religion is Giving Way to Spirituality*, Oxford: Blackwell Publishing.

Hesse, Douglas, 2009, 'Imagining A Place for Creative Nonfiction', *The English Journal*, 99.2, pp. 18–24.

Hill, Christopher, 1988, *A Turbulent, Seditious and Factious People: John Bunyan and his Church*, Oxford: Oxford University Press.

Ivens, Michael, 1998, *Understanding the Spiritual Exercises: Text and Commentary: A Handbook for Retreat Directors*, Leominster: Gracewing.

Kaufman, Gordon, 1993, 'Reconstructing the Concept of God', in David Pailin and Sarah Coakley (eds), *The Making and Remaking of Christian Doctrine: Essays in Honour of Maurice Wiles*, Oxford: Clarendon Press, pp. 95–115.

Kaufman, Gordon, 1995, *An Essay on Theological Method*, Atlanta, GA: American Scholars Press.

Kim, Sharon, 2006, 'Edith Wharton and Epiphany', *Journal of Modern Literature*, 29.3, pp. 150–75.

Latour, Bruno, 2005, *Reassembling the Social: An Introduction to Actor-Network Theory*, New York and Oxford: Oxford University Press.

Lee, Hermione, 2005, *Body Parts: Essays in Life Writing*, London: Chatto & Windus.

Leigh, David, 2000, *Circuitous Journeys: Modern Spiritual Autobiography*, New York: Fordham University Press.

Lindholm, Charles, 2013, 'The Rise of Expressive Authenticity', *Anthropological Quarterly*, 86.2, pp. 361–95.

Lyotard, Jean-François, 1984, *The Post Modern Condition: A Report on Knowledge*, trans. Geoff Bennington and Brian Massumi, Manchester: Manchester University Press.

MacIntyre, Alasdair, 1988, *Whose Justice? Which Rationality?*, Notre Dame, IN: University of Notre Dame Press.

Magro, Maria, 2004, 'Autobiography and Radical Sectarian Women's Discourse: Anna Trapnel and the Bad Girls of the Revolutions', *Journal of Medieval and Early Modern Studies*, 34.2, pp. 405–37.

McFague, Sallie, 1993, *The Body of God: An Ecological Theology*, London: SCM Press.

Miller, Daniel, 2010, *Stuff*, Cambridge: Polity Press.

Nussbaum, Felicity, 1989, *The Autobiographical Subject: Gender and Ideology in Eighteenth-Century England*, Baltimore: Johns Hopkins University Press.

Nye, David, 1996, *American Technological Sublime*, Cambridge, MA: MIT Press.

Pell, Barbara, 1998, *Faith and Fiction: A Theological Critique of the Narrative Strategies of Hugh MacLennan and Morley Callaghan*, Waterloo, ON: Wilfrid Laurier University Press.

Rasmussen, Bryan, 2010, 'From God's Work to Fieldwork: Charlotte Tonna's Evangelical Autoethnography', *ELH*, 77.1, pp. 159–94.

Ricoeur, Paul, 1991, *A Ricoeur Reader: Reflection and Imagination*, ed. Mario Valdes, Hemel Hempstead: Harvester Wheatsheaf.

Santmire, Paul H., and Cobb, John Jr, 2006, 'The World of Nature According to the Protestant Tradition', in R. Gottleib (ed.), *The Oxford Handbook of Religion and Ecology*, Oxford: Oxford University Press, pp. 115–46.

Saunders, Max, 2010, *Self-Impression: Life-Writing, Autobiografiction, and the Forms of Modern Literature*, Oxford: Oxford University Press.

Shaw, Philip, 2006, *The Sublime*, London: Routledge.

Sissons, Larry, 1998, 'The Art and Illusion of Spiritual Biography', in G. Thomas Kauser and Joseph Fichtelberg (eds), *True Relations: Essays on Autobiography and the Postmodern*, Westport, CT: Greenwood Press, pp. 97–108.

Smart, Elizabeth, 1991 [1978], *The Assumption of the Rogues and Rascals*, London: Paladin.

Staude, John-Raphael, 2005, 'Autobiography as a Spiritual Practice', *Journal of Gerontological Social Work*, 45.3, pp. 249–69.

Swinton, John, and Pattison, Stephen, 2010, 'Moving Beyond Clarity: Towards a Thin, Vague, and Useful Understanding of Spirituality in Nursing Care', *Nursing Philosophy*, 11.4, pp. 226–37.

Taves, Ann, 2003, 'Detachment and Engagement in the Study of "Lived Experience"', *Spiritus: A Journal of Christian Spirituality*, 3.2, pp. 186–208.

Tilden, Norma, 2004, 'Nothing Quite Your Own: Reflections on Creative Nonfiction', *Women's Studies*, 33, pp. 707–18.

Traherne, Thomas, 1966, *Thomas Traherne: Poems, Centuries and Three Thanksgivings*, ed. Anne Ridler, Oxford: Oxford University Press.

Tredennick, Linda, 2011, 'Exteriority in Milton and Puritan Life Writing', *Studies in English Literature 1500–1900*, 51.1, pp. 159–79.

Valdés, Mario, 1991, 'Introduction', in Mario Valdés (ed.), *A Ricoeur Reader: Reflection and Imagination*, Hemel Hempstead: Harvester Wheatsheaf.

van Bright, Theilman J., 1938 [1660], *Martyr's Mirror*, Scottdale, PA: Herald Press.

Walton, Heather, 2007, *Imagining Theology: Women, Writing and God*, London: T&T Clark.

Walton, Heather, 2014, *Writing Methods in Theological Reflection*, London: SCM Press.

Weil, Simone, 2009, *Waiting on God*, London: Routledge.

BIBLIOGRAPHY

Wilson, Tarn, 2012, 'The Space Between Contradictions: An Examination of Meaning and Knowledge in Life Writing', *Life Writing*, 9.2, pp. 137–56.

Wordsworth, William, 1969 [1850], 'The Prelude', in *Wordsworth Poetical Works*, ed. Thomas Hutchinson, Oxford: Oxford University Press, pp. 494–583.

PART 2

Not Eden: A Work of Spiritual Life Writing

I

Growth

The new house had no garden so we had to make one.

My grandad took a large sheet of paper and plotted the earth on to a grid. Each square to be worked on in turn. He brought a huge wooden riddle to sift the soil and pull out the stones. With a sharp, pointed fork he attacked thick, twisted coils of roots and stacked them into a pile like trophies from a hunting expedition.

My father did not wish to riddle or to sift. He took the larger stones and built them into walls and steps and paths. He liked it that the garden was not level or regular to the eye. He worked with his spade to sculpt and shape. But the spade was also a weapon. It came down on the heads of moles and rats. This was not any longer a wild wood but Woodhill Drive. It was a cul-de-sac.

My mother did not labour long in the garden, but she made raids upon it when the men were not looking. She took the kitchen scissors and a carving knife to attack plants she did not approve of. These were usually ones her father-in-law had planted, and which she considered too conventional or rigid in their habits. My mother liked plants that were not easily domesticated. She scraped among the stones with a tablespoon and planted forget-me-nots, foxgloves and poppies. Mice and birds often took the seeds, and my grandad riddled many of the green shoots away. But once those tiny seeds are planted in a garden they will take hold. She also planted sea pinks all the way up beside the steep garden path, because it is a lovely plant and because its common name is 'Thrift'. Even in a cul-de-sac you should remember that your father wore no shoes as a child, when he earned pennies by running to place bets for builders.

Watching the grown-ups I learned that gardening is not a peaceable art and that it is best to go armed into the garden. This is the lesson. Growing things is a dangerous business.

And I myself already knew something about growth.

When I was four years old, I was playing in the lounge, while my mother was busy in the kitchen. I was not lonely. The wireless and I were talking.

'NOW', said the wireless lady, 'crouch down on the ground and curl up into a little ball.'

'Like this', I said, folded up as tightly as could be.

'When the music plays', she told me, 'start to open up. Move your fingers and twiggle your toes. Listen to the stretchy music and feel your roots growing into the ground and your body getting bigger and bigger, taller and taller.'

'Yes, yes I can!'

Feet on the red and purple carpet, hands reaching for the ceiling. I was growing like Alice. Why wait to be five or six, when I could grow up right now? But suddenly fear! Was this a holy way to grow? Would anybody know me anymore? Why did I let that lady with her nice voice and sweet music enchant me? She has swollen-me-up like the witch did to Hansel. And so, crying, the huge monster girl runs along the hall and into her mother's arms.

Yes, I am not foolish in my desires. I know that growth is a perilous thing. One of the reasons is that you cannot know in advance where the changes are leading or that the end will be better than the beginning.

It was very hot the night I stayed at my best friend's house. She is still my best friend. Her name is Chloe. We were playing a game in the big double bed. She was the horse, and I was the rider who sat on her back. She was a wild horse that would not be tamed, so she must throw me off. I was the skilful rider, and I clung on tightly. It was very hot, and so we took off our nightclothes. Now this is a very good game, and so we were laughing loudly; laughing and clinging to each other when her big sister came into the room.

'You filthy little beasts', said the big sister, 'I can see what you will end up like.'

I put on my nightie again, and they put me in another bed in another room. The sheets were cool and crisp, but I could not sleep, because I was too worried about what I would end up like.

Even my mother sometimes had her doubts about this, although she was the one who had borne me. We were listening to a serial on the wireless together. An exquisite lady was dying of consumption very slowly surrounded by wax-petalled flowers. Every week when we listened we cried. Then the woman died in the last episode. I didn't cry then, because I didn't think it was so sad at the end of the struggle.

'Do not be heartless, my child', said my mother through her tears. I thought about this and could see that maybe I was becoming so. But then perhaps it is best to be stonehearted if, as I feared, everyone now loved my little sister more than me.

Not that I would have wished to take from Ella the smallest ounce of anybody's love. She deserved it all. She was a shining little jewel. I never wore pink, but she was always pink and white. My dress tore, my plaits came loose, my socks could never stay up on my legs, but she was just right. I would never stop talking, but when a stranger spoke to Ella, she didn't say anything. Her eyes just grew bigger and bigger, and she stared at them. In our shared room I spoke to her of God. Every night I read her a chapter from the Bible – from the beginning, right through and without cheating. Every single begat and beget was faithfully recorded. Then we knelt down on the floor, and I said the prayers, because I was the eldest and Ella was shy. God smiled down and kissed us both goodnight.

When people won't talk to you, then you can always talk with God. The Spirit speaks back to you in a quiet way inside, but you cannot reach out and touch her. You can also speak to rabbits. They don't speak out loud either, but they are very nice to touch. If you clean out the hutch and place the pine-scented sawdust thickly on the floor and cover this with handfuls of hay, then the rabbit will be pleased. Very peaceful and happy. You can give her some dandelion leaves, and while she eats, you can stroke her ears or even rest your head very gently upon her back. She might nudge you with her nose, but she will not bite you, and the rabbit and the hay smell sweet.

I was whispering with the rabbits that Sunday evening, when Chloe came to fetch me.

Right at this moment she is walking down the path towards me. I am waiting for her to reach me, because I am not writing this from far away looking back at a lost girl who has now grown. I should say the nuisance-girl herself keeps placing bunches of weeds and wild flowers on my windowsill. She presses the flowers some boy has given her between the pages of my books. Often I feel that I am growing into her, not that she has grown up into me. That is another dangerous thing about growth. It is not at all a one-way process. Just now I am 13 years old and kneeling on the grass with my rabbits, and Chloe is walking down the path towards me. It is the day I put off my innocence and began to make my own way through the world.

Chloe came to fetch me, but I had to pretend that I didn't expect her. My mother had a horror of already-made plans and projects and timetables to such an extent that she was always reluctant to let me know even her most straightforward intentions. If I were to ask her on a Saturday whether she was going to town in the afternoon, she simply wouldn't tell me. I could listen to her getting ready upstairs, drawers, wardrobe, bedroom door, and still not be absolutely sure she was going to leave the house. You could never be quite certain. She was quite capable of taking off her coat, opening a book or going to bed.

Chloe knew about my mother and when I exclaimed 'Oh look, Chloe's come!', she took her cue and said, as if she had just picked the idea out of the air: 'I'm going to Kat's and I wondered if you would like to come with me?'

My mother was listening, of course, and rewarded Chloe with a smile. She was in no way fooled but enjoyed someone who could play her own games quite well. How dreadful to have children who wanted their futures all cut and dried and packaged. She sent us off with a blessing.

We were going to Kat's, because she and Janice were already there and boys were coming too. Sean was coming . . . maybe. He was the person I always most wanted to see, but if I met him on the street I would turn and hurry in the other direction. He was beautiful, blood running close under the skin, with a fragile, boy's beauty. It was because of him I was going to Carol's. She was someone I was not certain about; fun, but in a risky, pagan sort of way. She would speak first to boys on the street. She had phoned up Sean and asked him to come round that night with the others, and her parents were going out.

Kat and Janice were really the other pair, because Chloe and I were best friends together. Despite this we kept up the fiction that we were all equally fond of each other. This wasn't easy, especially as I nursed a secret grudge against Janice. After the night I had stayed at Chloe's, her parents became very cool to me and tried to encourage Janice, who was quite contrary to me, in my place.

They took her on holiday and to all those private places that had been for Chloe and me alone. We knew all the paths through the sand dunes and had marked them with stones and sea string. In the field next to where Chloe's parents had their caravan was a chestnut horse with a white patch on its nose. It could take a sugar lump, and you didn't feel its lips, only its warm breath on your hand. One year it had a foal, but when we came back in the spring it was gone. Only the mother was standing in her old place by the gate.

Luckily, Chloe had a true heart and every attempt to separate us only brought us closer together. It also suited my mother's contrariness to feed our friendship the more because teachers, Chloe's parents and informed onlookers knew, they could definitely see, that we were 'bad for each other'. So Chloe and I were together but for some purposes. It is good and necessary to have other people, and Kat and Janice were our next-best friends.

Kat and Janice, Chloe and I had made a plan. The boys did not know that we had made a plan to snare them. These boys had been around with us for many months, but never would they ask any of us out or try and see any of us alone. They were perfectly presentable. We would have liked to have gone with them, but they were always joking and kicking cans along in the street or playing table football at the youth club. Girls were not supposed to approach boys. You must always be waiting and seeing. This is not so much fun. Hours of energy wasted and no sweet trophies. We were sick of this, but as we couldn't, any of us, make the first move to any of them, we decided, all of us, to make the first move to all of them. We were going to suggest a kissing game.

The boys are challenged by the girls to see if they dare to play a kissing game. If a girl chooses your secret number, it is the rule you must kiss her, outside in the corridor, while the others play records in the front room. A kissing game is full of promises. It is like growing to music. Taking without waiting and getting from boys what you want from them. Stealing their kisses.

Of course, because of their pride they had to agree to play.

Some secret voice whispered Sean's number to me, and I didn't doubt it. When I led my prize to me, his sweet cheeks were pink, and he was shy to meet my eyes. He smelled of grass and fields. He was tall and so he bent to meet me. Awkwardly, like a boy. His lips were firm and dry, and he kissed and kissed me. The others started to whistle and cough, but he smiled, and I kissed him; leaning against the coats hung in the corridor with our hands intertwined. That was the first night of all, but we played the kissing game all through the summer and on into the autumn. I kissed all the boys and he kissed all the girls but I thought he liked me best. With so much practice I was a good kisser for my age.

2

Blossoms

In our new house everything was very carefully chosen, saved for and modern. The wallpaper, the washing machine, the carpets and the cups all mixed in well together. They settled down and were at home.

But a dress hung in my mother's new wardrobe that she never wore. The dress did not fit easily into its hanging space. It had a full, full skirt. This was stiffened with sewn-in netting, and when the door opened, the skirt unfurled and blossomed out. There was a faint scent to it too. The dress was made from sateen cotton. The background was white, and it was patterned all over with huge red roses. The roses were not scarlet, and neither were they crimson red. They were as deep and as dark as blood.

I adored the dress. I asked my mother why she did not want to put it on. It was so lovely.

'That dress', she said, 'is special.'

'Can I have it if you don't want it?'

'No you cannot. Just because I don't wear it any more does not mean it has no use for me. And anyway you are a young girl, and this is not a dress for a girl to wear.'

I knew that this was true.

My mother was beautiful. Her hair was ash blonde, her lipstick was frosted sugar. Her skin was pale and flawless. She wore shifts or shirt-dresses, miniskirts, slacks, polo necks – and she had saved for a pair of Mary Quant shoes. Her earrings were daisies, and if ever a flower appeared on her clothing, it was simple and with open petals. Not ever a dark red rose.

So it seemed as if we were living in a happy, daylight world of soft dolly mixture colours. The special dress was too complicated and had no proper place here – apart from where it was hung. Squeezed into its narrow, dark casing. But this was only half the truth of the world.

In fact things were very changeable.

One day my mother came to collect me after school. She had dyed her hair in the time I had been sitting in my yellow classroom. And now it was auburn. Fiery and lovely. I knew it was her. I could see her waiting behind the wire fence in her usual place and wearing her trench coat with the collar turned up, and I could see her bright new hair. But I told the teacher:

'My mummy has not come.'

I said this even though it was not true. I was waiting for someone who was bleach-soft blonde. I was not waiting for a redheaded woman. I wanted her to stay the same, but she never would.

I don't think that this was her fault exactly.

She told me that when she was a girl she had sat with her own mother one bright spring day, and they had made flowers from tissue paper. They were not small or delicate blooms but as big as tea plates. And they had hung them all around the living room, so that it had blossomed like a tropical paradise. Like the hothouses in Canal Gardens at Roundhay Park. There were more flowers in that wee space than in Leeds market. They had made the flowers because her mother loved life, and gaiety, and every colourful, fantastic thing. But she was too ill to go outside anymore and enjoy the real flowers coming into bloom. And soon after she was too ill to do anything anymore, and her short, bright time was over. And my poor mother was just 14 years old.

So then came the years of the dancing and the lovely dresses and the courting of the handsome young man. And the crying at night time and the long blank days in which the sun never rose. It was never one thing or the other. Never just the sunshine or just the shadows. It was always a mixture of the things. Such a beautiful dress and the strong, slim fiancé with his dark hair and white shirts and shining shoes, his hand on her elbow – gentle. Going to the seaside and walking arm in arm along the pier. Tennis on a Saturday afternoon. Cinema and hotel dances and creeping in through the bathroom window of the Nurses' Home after the front door was locked. And the great aching longing that came at night, in the silence.

I went to my parents' room, because I could hear her crying, and she took me into the bed with her and taught me some words to sing:

Jesus bids us shine with a small, clear light
Like a little candle burning in the night
In this world of darkness so we must shine
You in your small corner and I in mine.

This is a simple, sweet song, but it is also funny. The small corner is where we naughty girls must sit. It made us laugh as we sang it, and she was not crying anymore. But the next night she was again. And many nights after. I thought that something was demanded of me. Some act or gesture that would make things better. But I could not think of anything to do. So every night after I read the Bible chapter I prayed. 'Dear God, please make my mummy happy.' And then, because I realized that of course mothers often do die, even when you need them, I also prayed a prayer that was really for me. 'Please keep her safe.' Then I put the Bible under my pillow, so that I would be protected in the night, and tried to sleep.

Those were my prayers. The prayers of a child who is too young for a world of night flowers. When I turned 14 in the year of the kissing game, my thoughts about many things began to change.

I stood at the top of our steep garden path. Evening was falling, and I could see the lights on in our lounge and in the windows of the rows of new houses spreading out below me. Beyond them I looked down towards the woods, all in darkness now, and rising past them, in the distance, was the horses' field. Its edges were rimmed with the gold and red of the sunset.

I was tired. I had been doing my paper round and carrying a heavy canvas sack full of the *Yorkshire Evening Post* from house to house. But I did not rush to go into my warm, bright home. I stood at the top of the garden looking out into the embers of the day.

The big bag on my shoulder was empty now and light. And I was also feeling a weight starting to lift from me. Tonight was youth club night. I was excited, fearful, longing. There would be no kissing games with all the grown-up helpers standing round – but there would be loud music in a dark room where the girls danced and Sean would be playing ping pong and table football in the games hall next door. And perhaps he might say something to me. He had started, sometimes, to say things just to me. Little bits of sentences only. But, nevertheless, this was unusual behaviour for a boy. Maybe this week something else might happen?

Even if it did not, this is being alive I thought. This is really being alive. Standing at the top of this steep path with all the light and darkness spreading out before me. How much more wonderful is this excitement and discomfort than the little comforts of childhood. And then, all at once, looking towards the horizon and the lovely purple evening sky, I realized that the prayers I said each night, and which echoed continually in my head by day, were silly. I had all at once outgrown them. Of course, you have only to look around you to see that God does not make people either happy or safe. Whatever business God is about it isn't that one. It clearly is not that one.

This new vision did not make me sad at all. I was elated. It was as if someone had whispered, very especially to me, an important clue. I had been given the information I needed to make sense of a very difficult puzzle that otherwise would keep me enthralled for ever. With this knowledge I could move on. I did truly feel as if a surprising but wholly satisfying answer had been given to my prayers and that I was free of the need to pray them over and over again. I was light and glad to run down the garden path, to wash my hands and sit at the table and eat my tea and laugh with Ella and try to do my French vocab all at the same time. Then I went upstairs to get ready.

Everything was fitting together. I had new black shorts to wear – tight fitting – and I thought they made me look like a dancer. My mother came up the stairs and knocked on the bathroom door. She was holding her pink Biba shirt – the loveliest shirt in the world – and she handed it to me to put on. When I arrived at the youth club, Kat just stared at me.

'You look fantastic', she said, 'Are you drunk?'

'No!' I laughed. But I felt as if I was.

We spent most of the evening in the corridor between the hall and the dancing room. Sometimes we went in to see the boys playing their games, and sometimes we went into the dark room to dance. The last song of the night was always for smooching, and the room was always empty when that was played, because it seemed rather sad for us girls just to dance with each other to the slow music. But this night, just as Maggie May started to play, the boys came into the corridor, and we all went into the dark room together.

No one had just one partner. We were used to sharing! We danced some time with one boy, and then we switched to another. My head rested on each shoulder in turn. Sean held me a little away from him, not close, but when I looked at him, he was looking at me and smiling. Kat went to the hatch where the DJ was watching and made him play the record again. And once more. Nothing like that had ever happened before.

After the music was turned off and we had to leave, we were all still together. It was quiet in the street. We linked arms and walked along the middle of the road. Sean was on one side of me, and Chloe was on the other. I was at the centre of the whole turning universe. I could hear the song of the Spirit sounding out across the starry heavens and all along the darkling plain.

3

Blight

The first flowers of the spring do not usually bear fruit. There is the show and the scent, but very rarely do they set fruit. The petals do not get ragged and worn, as they protect what grows inside. They fall quickly to the ground, before they have lost their first fresh beauty.

On my tenth birthday I was sick and had a headache. In the night I started to shake and could not stop shaking. Bright colours flashed across the dark room. It was measles, and I could not bear to eat or drink or look into the light. There was fear in my mother's face as she raised my boneless body to smooth the sheets beneath me. But then I began to get better, and the curtains were opened again. In the light summer evenings my mother lay next to me on the bed and read from *Little Women*. It is Beth who is the best of all the sisters. She embroiders special flowers, tiny pansies called Heartsease, and the stitches are to take away all the pain in the world. But Beth is the sister who has to die, and it is Jo who looks back sadly but goes on living. There are many things that are beautiful and good, but some of these cannot survive beyond childhood.

I was in the garden. Upstairs on a coat-hanger hung my green and black skirt and white blouse together with the black waistcoat that reached right to the bottom of the skirt. These were the clothes I had chosen for next time we would play the kissing game. But at that moment I was wearing the clothes of a child not to be seen in public. My hair was in two long plaits, and I was with the rabbits. Chloe came down the path looking more beautiful than I had ever seen her; she wore a short light-grey skirt and a fluffy white jumper. She had white boots. But here I was in all the grubbiness of childhood. She had brought me chocolate like a gift for a child. Why?

So the April wind blows and the flower falls; so the frost comes in the night and the flower falls; so it is too warm in the spring, and the plant has grown too quickly to be strong and the flower falls.

I stayed away from school. My parents were working, and Ella did not tell. There was no one but me in the house for all the long days, but I did not read and I did not listen to the plays on the wireless in the afternoon. I had a record and took the arm off the record player, so that it played over and over again. The woman kept singing the same words, and I tried to believe them:

Where's your smile today?
Try and see, she didn't mean to make you feel so sad.

Chloe and Sean were both tall, slim and fair. They matched perfectly, and they were lovely to look at together. She went with him to places I had never been. It seemed that her clothes were all new, she looked completely different. When I returned to school, she brought me presents every day, but they were presents to a child, and they sickened me. I could almost forget when we were sitting together and talking in sign language with our hands all through the lessons. But things could not be the same.

That was the first blight, but the second was worse.

Kat and Janice and I decided that it was best to go out with boys, for practice, even if you didn't like them very much. You could always swap if a better one came along later. So, while Chloe walked tall beside Sean, I walked beside Michael who was rather too short: he wore an army great coat, but it had to be taken up at the hem. When he kissed, he sucked my lips in, so that I began to wonder whether this sort of practice might in the end be worse than no kissing practice at all.

Then Chloe stopped going with Sean, but she didn't come back to me either in the old way – although she still loved me, and her notes to me in class were pages long. Chloe was always wild at the edges, but there was something in her wilder now, and she was looking for wild boys. It was as if she and Sean had made each other drunk, and although they weren't together anymore, they both had the same sort of look on their faces. I wasn't shame-cheeked like them, but I still wanted him.

It was at a party, and because my eyes were shining and my hair was loose and I had been drinking beer, he thought I was like him.

'You've changed', he said. 'You've really changed.'

But I hadn't. He just couldn't see me. He liked to kiss me, well, he'd always liked to kiss me, only this time it wasn't alone in the corridor we did it; it was in a dark room where lots of couples lay in each other's arms. In the next days we kissed a lot, and sometimes I saw him screwing up his eyes, because he could tell in the light that I wasn't the same as him.

I think there was only one good day. Sharp and crisp like a green apple. He came around at 8.00 a.m. on a Saturday morning. He'd been out fishing since before light and was not wild at all but happy and tired. It was the bittersweetest summer morning, and so we walked along by the stream between the trees. In these woods were some houses made from planks of wood, and their roofs were covered with rolls of tarpaper like rabbit hutches. People used to stay in these houses sometimes at weekends. They were not young people, and they were sitting out in the sunshine drinking tea that day, and they waved to us. We kissed in the long grass, where we could not be seen, and he gave me a dog rose from a tangled bush. These are strange flowers; like poppies they melt if you pick them. Standing in water doesn't help them either. Pink turns to grey.

My kissing was not enough to keep him. My breasts weren't enough for a wild boy like him. They were white and round but the nipples were small and pink. Just buds, not flowers to suck out sweetness from. There were awful long hours of struggle – holding close and pushing away at the same time. If you know it's dying it doesn't help at all – especially if you are so young and you feel as if you are dying too. Each day you wake up and think it is going to be today.

The hardest thing about it all was that he sent Kat to tell me. That was not kind.

I should say that Kat was not wild, and yet she wasn't tied up like me with big fears and hopes and inside struggles. She had never had strings to break, but without them she still usually walked in the line unless there was a reason to step outside it. She did step outside it when she took Sean for herself a few weeks later; but then he tamely came to follow her, walking in step. He lost his wildness and his young boy's beauty in the year he was with Kat. I suppose that he might have been able to stay beautiful, but it probably would have killed him. All his strength would have had to go into that quick bright time. Instead, he grew up, left school and got a job which was as he wanted, and so he is today.

What was I to do?

My mother saw me crying. What was she to say?

4

Rootbuds

There are some plants that don't grow and spread themselves by setting seeds at all. They don't need the bees and the long calm summer days. They find it easier to send up new shoots from their roots underground. The roots run good and deep so the plant can survive when the frost blackens all the leaves. Growth comes out of their stored-up strength hidden in the ground. Well, the plants seem to do well, so does it matter?

Alongside Chloe, Kat and Janice, I had another friend, and she was someone rare and precious. Not everyone is lucky enough to have a friend like this. Her name was Sybil, and that was strange in itself, because she was half Chinese and half Czech, so where could she have found a name like Sybil? Because of her name she was already special.

Chloe and I stole her. It was our first day at high school, and already we had formed the pact with Janice and Carol from little-school days. We had to choose seats, and quickly all four of us made for the window side of the room away from the teacher's desk. We sat in a line. There were five places on this side, and Sybil had the other one. The teacher explained to us that Sybil needed a special friend because her family had escaped over borders chased by the secret police and the Russian soldiers. She couldn't speak English.

'Who will volunteer?'

All four of us put our hands up, but the teacher didn't choose us. She chose a nice girl called Hilary. Really a nice girl, very witty, we liked her. But we wanted Sybil for ourselves, and so we stole her from her friend Hilary.

I brought her books to help her with her English reading. Chloe made soft and lovely things for her on her mother's sewing machine, because Sybil hardly had anything of her own. They did not have time to pack all they needed when they left in a hurry. One Saturday all four of us caught the bus to her house and spent the afternoon there. Sybil showed us the pictures that she had made from cutting out paper. The paper was red, and she had cut tiny slivers out with a scalpel and stuck the lace dragons and cherry blossom on to a white background. This is a very Chinese art.

Sybil was pleased to be our friend. Not only because of our kindness, but because we were also the most interesting and naughty girls in the class. We didn't hang around the playground at break. We found secret places to go. In the room where the cleaners kept their buckets and mops there was a cupboard in the wall. If you walked into the cupboard, you could see another little door in the back of it, and this led into the tunnels made for cables and heating pipes that went under the school.

There were hundreds of tunnels, and they even joined the buildings of the girls' school with the building of the boys' school next door. You could climb out of the tunnel at other points, not just through the cupboard – but also under the school stage and in one of the storerooms by the biology lab. When someone stumbled over a cable and all the lights in the school fused, they had to find out why, and so we were caught climbing out, all covered in dust. So that was that. But we had some wonderful times in those tunnels, and Sybil came with us.

She was with us all the time at school, but although, after the first few months, she moved closer to where we lived in the new houses next to the woods, it still wasn't very near. It was better though, because we could go visit her without having to catch a bus on Saturdays. As usual Janice, Kat, Chloe and I went together.

First, I would walk up the hill to call for Janice. Janice had three sisters, and they slept two to a bed in one room and argued all the time. This was very different from the deep and sweet talking that I had with Ella, but I was still jealous of her in a way. All the girls seemed to be the same age. In their room tights were hung on clothes hangers to dry, talcum powder made a fine dust covering everything, and there were copies of the best magazines telling 'My True Story' of 'Real Life Romance'. Janice would always be ready and want to get away from her sisters as soon as possible. She thought I was very innocent. She had a kind heart and tried to look after me. She gave me cigarettes, because I never had any money.

Next we reached Chloe's house. Chloe was the only one now her sister had left home, and her parents were usually somewhere else. Chloe stayed up late in the night. She made beautiful clothes and practised make-up techniques like drawing flowers and stars on her face. In the daytime she was tired. Janice and I made the coffee, and Chloe put on the record player to get dressed to. We had a cigarette before we set off.

'Oh God', said Chloe, 'is that the time already?'

Kat's place was the last, and Kat's bedroom overlooked the long road we would have to walk up to Sybil's. She would have been watching from the window for a while, and she always knew if we might meet some boys on the road. I remember this very well when the roads were dangerous because of boys.

On many Saturdays we made this journey to Sybil's, and at school we were always together. But the kissing game was something that Sybil didn't have much share in. The boys all wanted to kiss her, and for a very short while she joined in – convincing herself that this was just a game like the 'kiss, dare, truth or promise' we used to play behind the tennis courts at school. But she wasn't often allowed out at night, and something in her was shamed by employing the turn-taking and chance of children's games as a licence to hold close or pull away. Of course, we wanted to tell her everything about the times she missed and describe each turn to her, but it's hardly the same if you can't feel the smoothness of your lips after they have been hard kissed. We were flowering in a quick succession of bright blossoms, but Sybil was growing in a different way, and in my still, almost lifeless, time she showed me this other way.

Despite the secret police and the soldiers from which he had fled, Sybil's father was still a communist, and her brother was a communist too. The brother was the only other person I knew who had read the whole Bible. But he didn't read it kneeling down at night with prayers, but in those few spare moments he took for relaxation, while he was studying equations and elemental tables for his A levels. He said this reading was a change from physics and essential to gain a proper understanding of European culture. He was dark and sweet and inspiring, this elder brother of Sybil. His father shared with him the faith of his heart and all the pains of exile. He also spent the empty days searching the secondhand bookshops and the cardboard boxes in the market stalls, buying books for his son if they were important and should be read. This brother then thought Sybil should read the books too, even though she was still young, because what could matter more? Sybil passed the books to me, because I liked to read, and especially I liked to share a secret world with Sybil.

Then Sybil's brother went away to university. I liked it best when he was away because, gentle as he was, he made me clumsy, tongue-tied and awkward. He always wanted to know my opinion about things it had never occurred to me there were opinions about. Most of all I liked him being away, because we could sit in his room when I went to visit Sybil in the evenings. Those evenings when she was not allowed out, and I did not want in my heart to go out to girls' and boys' places.

All the rooms in Sybil's house were interesting. The sitting room was not furnished with a three-piece suite like every other home I knew, but with lots of comfy chairs that didn't match. There was a study instead of a dining room. This was piled up with books in German, Chinese and French. The proudest of all these were the German volumes of Marx just above the desk. The shelf sagged in the middle with the weight of them. I always tried to peep into the study if the hall door was open, but it was the brother's room that was the best.

The floor had straw matting that must be kept supple by watering it with an enamel watering can. The bed was Chinese and could be folded away, but it was usually open like another mat upon the floor. The bedspread was of rough woven cotton, and there were no curtains but bamboo blinds, instead, and piles of books and a record player and a poster of Marx with his beard and Mao Tse Tung and Che Guevara:

> Che is dead but his memory lives on,
> In the hearts of the masses and the
> Masses will inherit the earth.

We knew that Che is not a name like Christ is not a name. It is a title given, and it means 'friend'. Che was called 'friend' because he was the lover of the people and, like Christ, he was betrayed and killed.

'I am just a man like you but the revolution is immortal', he told the cowards who came to shoot him.

The imperialists did it, the foreign bankers and the landlords. The tyrants and the murderers. It was because of the land, the earth, the people's treasure. This we read all about in one of the books. The heroic tragedy of Che with the blurry photos of his body after the execution that might have been very horrifying, but luckily were not very clear.

We also read *The Communist Manifesto* and *To the Finland Station*, *Ten Days That Shook the World* and *The Rise and Fall of the Third Reich*. And there were other books that belonged with them, right at the heart of it, because of the European culture. European culture in my small world with the bedroom I shared with Ella, and it overlooked the small new houses by the side of the wood.

Le Grand Meaulnes is a very peculiar book, and I don't think I got it, although I read it twice because Sybil liked it. *The Little Prince* is lovely and with pictures like *The Fairy Tales of Oscar Wilde*. Balzac is rude and smelly like Maupassant too – but you want to read them because even in the sunshine they take you into the secret stuffiness of struggles in closed chambers. And Dickens is better when you read the books than when you watch the stupid serials on television. Lovely and lovely is *The Rubaiyat of Omar Khayyam*:

> The moving Finger writes, and, having writ,
> moves on; nor all your Piety nor wit
> shall lure it back to cancel half a Line,
> Nor all your Tears wash out a Word of it.

You say this in your head like you say:

> This the true measure of love:
> when we believe that we alone have loved. That
> no-one would have loved in this way before us
> and no-one will love in the same way after us

from Goethe. Or,

> O fat white woman whom nobody loves
> Why do you walk through the fields in gloves.

All these words are magic spells to ward away evil and sadness.

Teachers don't like you to read things like this. Particularly, they don't like it if you read them while they are teaching you at the time. They become very angry. They prefer it if you pass notes or throw balls of paper with a bent ruler. It would be better to eat sandwiches or do your homework. They would rather you gave your neighbour a black eye than that you read a book.

That is most teachers, but some are different. Our history teacher was a complicated, clever, crumpled man. He had been to Oxford and never taken off his gown. He often recited to us a poem in which a child discovers a human skull. He asks his grandfather where it has come from and is told a tale of a mighty battle, clashing forces, a great victory and an awful defeat. The child listens. Then he speaks his important question:

'"But what good came of it at last?" Quoth little Peterkin.'

'That', said our history teacher, 'is what you must always ask. Whenever you hear of anything in the world. Its pomp and circumstance and vain glory. You must ask: "What good came of it at last?" Oh, you girls. Don't grow up to be bun bashers and baby boomers. Say, "What good came of it all?" What good will come of it all?'

I was in history class, and I was reading some short stories by Somerset Maugham, when the teacher came up behind me and grabbed the book.

'What's this? What's this? W. Somerset Maugham. Yes. Finest prose writer in English. I see. Literature is the sweet dessert wine of the intellect. Well done. Well done.'

He gave me the book back and patted my head. I didn't myself like Somerset Maugham very much, but I could hardly say this, when he had been so nice about it.

With these books and with Sybil I was discovering that love has a proper place; romantic love I mean, loving a boy so that you feel ill and can't do things. It is like being drunk. When you are drunk, that sweeps you off your feet, but then in the morning you have to get up and walk to the bus stop by the wood.

The skies are grey, and the big double willow tree sways in the wind, and there is a more refreshing feeling that is called 'blessed normality'. I lean on the bus stop or sit on the kerb and say 'blessed normality'. Of course, by the evening you want the drinking and the dancing and the touching again. But this must have its proper place. The world is very big and this is very small.

Because I did not have a boyfriend and was reading a lot, my friend Janice's mother was puzzled by me. One day she said: 'Do you know what it feels like to be in love and stay up all night?' I wanted to say: 'I know what it's like to be in love with a line of poetry, to ache and be sleepless with questions.'

But this was not the sort of reply I could give her as the rock and roll music played and Janice's sisters jived with all the proper steps in the next-door room just as she had taught them. I loved the music, old as it was and the records scratched and bald, but I couldn't do all the proper steps and move in the easy way they did.

5

Nature and Grace

When I was very little what I wanted to believe was that where our wood stood there had always been a wood. So when the line of new houses grew thicker and the wood smaller, it was as if the whole of the ancient world was threatened. I lived in a new house, but to me it was an old house, and I hated the new houses that were still being built next to the horses' field, by the stream. They wanted to run some of the stream through pipes. They had unloaded the huge pipes already in the place where the boys used to play cricket.

I stood by the tallest oak tree and put my fingers in the deep grooves of the bark; the rough bark which so often scraped my flesh:

Oak Trees,
Skin your knees.

I was grieving for something the tree did not know about yet. It no longer ruled its own kingdom. If it was lucky, it might be left standing in someone's new back garden, but it would be tamed and confined and its lower braches sawn off. I gathered acorns from the ground and plucked mysterious, wooden oak apples from the lower branches.

Further up the bracken path stood twin crab apple trees. Their lovely arms were strong and open, and their grey limbs were skin smooth. These trees told me an unwelcome secret. Twin trees like these don't just appear in a wood by chance. Nor was the thicket of raspberry canes towering high over our heads a prehistoric accident. The vigorous blue and lilac lupins self-seeded but they were out of place if this were a virgin forest.

What I then knew, but still did not wish to admit, was that people had been in this place before we came. Not only had they made paths and planted kitchen gardens, the woods also had buildings in them. That is, there were the ruins of buildings where people lived before. When I climbed over the place where the old wall dipped, I was not entering an innocent wilderness where nothing had ever happened. It was just the same in the wood as everywhere else in the world. There was a confusion and a conflict of powers. Our lovely wood was not the first innocent chaos but the later fallen and fruitful one.

I was playing in the woods, when I was startled by a cockerel staring full into my face, his neck was stretched out to crow and his horny beak wide open. The cockerel was fierce and beautiful with russet brown and blue and black feathers; raised up to confront me it stood nearly as tall as I was, and we looked into each other's eyes.

The cockerel and his hens were the last of the stock belonging to an old lady who lived in a small white cottage with a millpond in front. Some of our wood was really the last few fields of her smallholding; overgrown with brambles and the walls all falling down. I stood with other children and watched the lady leaving her house for the last time. She was very old and leaned on the arm of her old son. The front door was locked and never opened again, but we children climbed in through the back windows and made the cottage our own.

Yes, it is best to acknowledge this. There will always be someone else arriving and demanding their turn. The moving process is ruthless, and it is unstoppable. Step down into the garden, my darling, for see now your apples are ripe.

On the day when we moved into our new house, I had sat high in the cab of the removal lorry, and when we arrived, I stepped down very solemnly to claim my allotted inheritance. There were no roads then, only pavements with kerb stones standing high above cinder-bedded tracks. The car tyres crunched in the mornings and evenings, when people left for work or returned home to rest. The bus stop had been built already, near the big double willow tree, but the bus could not yet reach it and had to stop next to the old station. The bus stop's new sign was covered by an old coal sack to show that there was no point leaning against the concrete pole and waiting.

It was in this half-begun and half-ended space we were making our garden.

When he had fashioned the paths and garden walls, when the old stumps and rubble had been removed, my father felt that more was needed than my grandfather's dahlias and tea roses or my mother's semi-civilized flowers. He started to bring the woods into barren ground the builders had left us. He took his wheelbarrow and slung his spade over his shoulder and strode out to see what he could find. Whole trees staggered stiffly down the cinder road and climbed over our gate. There was a rowan tree, and my father said that this was for my mother. It was young now, but soon it would be as tall as the house and hung with berries for the birds in winter. Rowan trees were to protect the home and all who lived there. They were guardian spirits. For me he planted a silver birch, the maiden tree, slender, light and supple. Always the first to grow again when ground was cleared. When Ella was born at Christmastime, he celebrated with a shop-bought conifer. Sweet smelling and perfect it looked timid and tiny in its plant pot but soon naturalized, growing a foot a year, losing its nursery neatness and finding its place among the rest.

He did not need to carry in the lupins. They came themselves and settled in alongside the foxgloves. Even the builders had not managed to root out the bluebells, and among these each year we planted our Christmas hyacinths – their cultivated cousins. Our plants were exiles and migrants moving from cultivation to the wild and back again. This gardening that was sweet disorder, and I had my own contribution to make.

I took the soft green sprouting potatoes from the bottom of the sack and planted them very carefully in the flowerbeds between daffodils and wallflowers. My acorns all developed into perfect little trees, but only one was allowed to remain in the garden. The others were tenderly wrapped in damp newspaper and taken back to be planted in the wood – but in a place that was safe from the diggers and the lorries. Best of all were the cherry trees I grew from the stones of cherries in our tinned fruit salads. These tins had come all the way from Australia, and out of the many I planted two grew and stood each side of the gate. They matured along with me and surprisingly soon carried white blossom in spring and smooth, exotic lemon and pink cherries in the summer.

It was a sunny afternoon, and I stood alone in the wood collecting blackberries, catching them while they were still firm and purple and filling the large jar I had brought with me. I scratched my arms reaching for the best berries right at the top, but each one of these was a special triumph. At home I put the berries into a small cardboard carton I had covered with silver foil. In the morning I carried this carefully up the hill to the new church. Ella brought two red apples resting on a bed of blue tissue paper.

The harvest festival was fantastic and frightening. It was plenty but also danger. 'All is safely gathered in', but be careful and bar the doors quickly for soon 'the winter storms begin'. What we had brought seemed good and wholesome, but in the wild world around it was not so easy to tell whether what was growing was the right thing in the right place. The wheat and weeds were all together sown and soon, following their own natures, would be 'into joy or sorrow grown'.

I was enjoying all the ripeness and the danger, when I saw the Minister crossing over to where my small silver box had been placed, and he raised it up to show the congregation. I was embarrassed, because the other girls had all brought shop fruit, and some of their mothers had wrapped their gifts in cellophane.

'This', he said, 'is the type of fruit that God desires. The fruit of our love and our labours.'

I was very glad that God liked my blackberries, but remained puzzled as to why something growing wild that I had gathered was to be preferred to fruit that had been carefully chosen, paid for and wrapped up nicely. I thought myself that the berries looked rather out of place now in the church. It was only a small box, and black juice was beginning to seep through the tin foil.

And then the year turned and turned again.

We ourselves, into joy and sorrow grown, became the harvest of the fields of God.

Chloe and I were kneeling with the others by the communion rail, and we were making promises. It was Easter Sunday morning – the spring before the summer of the kissing game. This day both of us had white dresses, but hers was short and lacy and mine was not. We made the promises as we had practised, and we believed them. If you meant what you said in your heart, then you would become someone very special and different. But somehow the words we were saying only made sense within those walls. In the afternoon, still wearing our white dresses, we went paddling in the millpond.

Then Chloe did not go to church with me anymore.

It was a winter evening and already dark. I set off from home carrying my small radio, so that I could hear what the new number one single was at 7 o'clock. I had to know this before I went in to the church, so I hid round the side wall hoping no one would see me and drag me into the lighted porch to welcome me. I was a few minutes late, because I liked the song and listened right to the end. But in the evening service no one minded very much. It was not the devout who came to this church at night.

When I entered the quiet sanctuary, I looked around with kindness at the people. I had tenderness towards the shy soft-spoken man who wore yellow socks. I blessed my former Sunday school teacher, a handsome, deeply doubting man, holding his bowed head in his hands. I was grateful for the evening lady who was playing the piano. Her hands were arthritic, and the piano sounded wistful when she played it. I was glad she was not the daylight organist who pumped away too cheerfully at the pedals and drowned out all our longings.

The preacher we had that night was a man I liked. He had been having a sustained argument with God for many years, and I could see merit on both sides.

I now belonged with these evening-service people, sitting in my own place on the back row and never in a white dress now. We might look like accidental attenders blown in by the wind. And in a way that would be true. But in fact we were the ones who left our homes to come out at night in answer to an unlikely invitation. We were the surprising guests at the great feast. The unexpected harvest.

Yet despite being so safely gathered in, the cares of the world were still pressed down upon me.

'Oh God', I prayed, 'please don't let me get pregnant', and, 'please, please let me go to university.'

You should be very careful indeed what you pray for.

6

The Fruit You Shall Not Eat

I had a little nut tree
Nothing would it bear
But a silver nutmeg,
And a golden pear.

I was late starting, and then two things happened at about the same time. I started bleeding regularly, reliably and painlessly. I also started to pass exams. Now I have won all the prizes and the only tests that I fail are driving tests and pregnancy tests. Whenever I take them, I don't expect to fail, having got into the habit of passing, but I do fail. Nevertheless.

The pregnancy tests on sale at the chemists offer you two windows on the world. Hold the test carefully and watch as a wash of brilliant colour moves across both these windows. Lovely colours. Deep pink sunset or turquoise blue wave. If, as the colours pass, they leave bars on each window, if you are completely locked in, then you are pregnant. If all the colour moves quickly from the first to the second window, and no bar appears, you are not pregnant. There is always a bar in the second window – this is for your own safety.

As the colours travel, I am always interested in following them. Then suddenly I am left looking through an open window. I am free to climb out and escape or just to sit and enjoy watching the world go by. Sometimes things can look slightly rose tinted or submarine after the test. That is an interesting perspective to have upon life that was not there before. Try to be glad about this, and be glad of your freedom and specialness of vision. Try not to cry for the whole day again this time. Do not attempt to retake the test immediately, in case the result was wrong and you have not really failed.

When we were in the fifth form, there was a deep hot summer. It began in June during our exams, and then the days stretched out. After the exams were finished, we didn't have to go back to classes. Janice would never go back; she was leaving to work in an office. Chloe would not go back either, because she was going straight to do a course at art college. Sybil and I were anxious for our results, because we wanted to stay on at school and then go to university. Kat had not decided what to do – she was going to wait and see.

Even though there were no more classes, I still woke every day at school time and looked around for something to do. I was trying to read Shakespeare, but the weather was too beautiful for the big thick book, and so usually I went to Chloe's and made her breakfast and tried to get her to talk to me. I was surprised that morning, because she was up and outside in the garden already. Lying in her bikini in the sun. Her arms were brown, her body was turning red, on her neck were deep love bites like crushed red and purple berries. She was not in a good mood, so I made some coffee and took one of her cigarettes. I rolled up my sleeves and lay back in the sun as well.

Then Chloe was crying. She was crying, because she had been with a boy from our next-door school. He was in the sixth form and tall and clever. Everyone liked him, and Chloe had wanted him for a long time.

'Why are you crying, if you got the one you wanted?'

'Because it is not like in the kissing game. I have found out that this is not the way it is in real life.'

The boy had pretended to Chloe. He pretended he had chosen her and that he was glad and happy to have her as his prize. Then later when she was lying with him, he had just got up and walked away. She saw him talking with his friends, and he was laughing. I spoke to Chloe about the art college and the new life and how she didn't have to see this horrible boy again and how nobody would find out what had happened. But they would, they certainly would. Spit on this boy for what he had done to Chloe.

My mother loved Chloe as if she were her own, and when she realized that she had been wounded, because Chloe wore her soul on the outside and never learned to hide it, she did not abandon her. We were going to the Highlands with people from my mother's church, and it was arranged that Chloe would come with us. We would stay in a castle (a small castle) with a swimming pool (outside) and a croquet lawn. In the morning we would all have breakfast at long tables, and there would be a huge teapot. We could sit in that sunny room for hours and drink cups of tea from the urn that never runs dry.

There were people, mostly related to me, who were the same age as Chloe and me. There was a room in the castle where we all gathered that used to be a conservatory and had a glass roof. This room was good on fine days, because it streamed with light. However, it was also good when it rained because the rain beat on the glass and you could see the texture of the raindrops on the roof. This was best at night when the moon managed to shine through the clouds with white rain light. Here we met to talk and listen to music, play table tennis. Here Chloe loved to sit and laugh at stupid jokes and beat the boys at table tennis and wrestle with them in a playing way. They were shy and giddy with fun. The same age as us and therefore much younger.

One evening we went for a walk. The air was moist with the rain that comes after a hot day; the heavy air was still. Our laughing, our singing and the darkness beginning to settle. They had been cutting hay in the fields and rolling it into huge cylindrical bales. We thought these were very neat, and we tried to roll them along but could not. The fields looked half finished with some of the hay standing and then the close-cropped parts.

The lane led between the fields and at the crossroads at the top of the hill was a telephone box. All ten of us managed to get in the phone box at once, Ella is so small and thin, so then we phoned the operator to let her know what we were doing. Chloe did this, and she was laughing and laughing.

All through the holiday Chloe wore make-up in the way she did at home, by herself, when she sat up late in the evenings. She had a perfect flower on her left temple, and the stalk curled down her cheek. Her mother might not have liked her to walk around like this, but everyone on the holiday thought it looked very good.

Chloe didn't spend all the time with me. She went for long walks with my uncle gathering wood for the barbecue and talking with him, although my uncle was an angry, awkward man who didn't usually talk much to anyone at all. She played bowls with the old ladies, bending over to throw the balls. Beautiful in a halter-neck top and all the bones standing out on her brown back as she bent over.

Chloe was so simple that fortnight, so quiet and gentle. She was on holiday from all the things that made her laugh, so fragile and her eyes so bright at home. She had grown downwards like a plant in winter to escape the frost.

I was simple and happy too because of another reason. Boys from France came to work at the castle for the summer, and one of them, dark curly hair, black cotton trousers, red espadrilles, cigarettes that smell of tar, he chose me for the late night walks and kisses. Simply kisses pressed to the warm castle walls where the honeysuckle grew. He was busy all day, and so he only came to me at night. He was a secret Latin lover with the softest lips, and he caused me no trouble or worry, only sweet dreams in the dormitory bed where I crept in the early mornings and with dreamy smiles over the morning tea. I must say by the end of the holiday I was very tired of the kissing nights, but it was so nice, French smoke kisses.

We came home, and a few weeks later Chloe went to college. I went back to school with Sybil. Kat came too, but she was going around with other friends now for most of the time. Perhaps it was because the summer had been so hot, but the autumn was brilliant. The silver birch trees in the playground by the sixth form block burned gold for weeks, and the skies

THE FRUIT YOU SHALL NOT EAT

were copper-sulphate blue. I spent a lot of time gazing out of the window, because I was unhappy. I missed Chloe who had sat beside me for ten years. The work should have been much more fun, but I didn't like the other sixth formers much. They had begun to make statements. They liked to make statements which were supposed to just hang in the air and not be laughed at like jokes or argued about like we argued over everything at home. I didn't know what to do with these things, so I just laughed and they got angry: either this or I got angry, then they laughed.

I had to separate myself. Most of these sixth formers had grown long hair and wore jeans. I pulled my skirts tight and wore high heels. My friend Sybil did not feel so out of place. She would happily join the circle of serious students and tried to help me do so too. She could talk to them without sharp and sarcastic swords being drawn. Without wanting to send arrows flying at them. I tried to be sweeter but couldn't be. I was unhappy but really the answer was simple.

In the sixth form they trust you not to skip away. This is moral blackmail and to be resisted.

So skip, skip, skip.

I went to college with Chloe.

There was a stool to sit on by her drawing board. All of the students had these desks with lids that could be raised and lowered with screws. They drew with charcoal and bright waves of water-colour paint. Sunset pink and turquoise blue. They drew light itself and concentrated hard to see it. Staring, without seeing, out of the huge windows of the studio. No one minded who came and went or which student went out for a coffee or a walk around the park to gather inspiration. No one minded if another person, small with dark hair, was sat on the stool reading or drafting an essay. There was music from a record player and all the students muttered to themselves; humming and moving backwards and forwards over their work like bees over flowers.

This is a quiet fertile hum. The best sound in the world to work to. Happy here to dream about the birth of the nation state or 'the pity of war/the pity war distils'. Happy here to consider supply and demand curves which criss and cross but don't show the living work of the worker. This is the invisible bar that the graph does not show, but you can see it if you concentrate hard enough. It is called surplus value and it is what Marx says keeps the workers' labour invisible. Economics is a mystical science.

Here everyone was patient with me and cared for me like an adopted child. Even the lecturers were gentle, when they said: 'We think you should leave for an hour or so, while we give this talk about printing techniques', or, 'This session about linear perspectives probably won't hold much of interest for you'.

I did not mind when I had to leave, because I had another place to go to.

Chloe shared her money with me. She gave me two cigarettes and some matches rolled in a twist of paper, and I went to the Italian café across the road. The tables were darkly polished wood, and the ones by the wall formed cubicles. The coffee making machine looked like a small silver power station and hissed and steamed. At night people came to eat exciting meals, but in the daytime it was coffee and magnificent sandwiches of Italian ham or Italian cheese. This is also European culture – like French kissing.

Always in my big bag were the books I needed for the schoolwork and the books for my own self. So here I read Simone de Beauvoir and found that she did her writing in a little bar in Paris. She lived in a hotel and came down every day to the bar and said to her friends:

> There is an indefinable loss in the spirit of our age and Sartre makes me cry in bed. I have decided never to bring a child into the world and believe I am a complete woman.

Then she has a drink and starts to write. This novel she is writing is about a young woman, whom Sartre strips with his eyes every time she walks into the bar.

'What a precious young thing she is', says Simone. 'Here is careless vitality and life.'

She smiles at her and calls her 'my dear'. Maybe she arranges to meet her later 'just us two'. And she writes a novel in which the older woman lover kills the young girl lover quite dead and gets away with it.

Then I used to smile to myself at the powerfulness of the girl. This was because I was the young girl who Simone was writing to death but could not kill. I think I must have been fertile then. I was certainly potent. Perhaps it was then I should have had my child. Then when everything was possible. But I was too busy sitting with the artists and looking out of the windows with them.

7

White and Red Roses

There was a widow (or so she said) who had two rose trees growing in her garden. One had white flowers and the other red. She also had two daughters. She called her daughters after these plants. They had no second names. Snow White liked to stay at home and read to her mother (I don't think so). Rose Red liked to wander freely through the woods and meadows (of course she did). Although they were different the sisters were best friends and loved each other very much. They also had a special affinity with animals. Some of these were small, timid furry creatures (baby bunnies and fawns). Others were not. Snow White married a big golden bear (prince) and Rose Red had to make do with his domesticated younger brother who had never snarled, growled or grown long fingernails. There is a moral in this story.

    The cross, grey teacher was never nice to us during the day and the only time we could relax was when we sat together on the coconut matting before home time and she read us a story. Her voice changed then, and as well as the wicked witch, she could be the good fairy. She had a collection of home-time stories that were kept on a high shelf above her desk. Among these were a set of square white books which were stories written by the brothers grim and glum. One day when I was looking up at these, she reached out and took a book down from the shelf and handed it to me without a word. She did not say anything to me while I was reading the story, and when she saw I had finished, she took it back and put it in its place again. Snow White and Rose Red. I could see that it was a story full of unanswered questions and dangerous contradictions.

Was it better to be the pure white sister or the deep red one? If a person looked at Chloe and me, they might have asked that same question. But then they would have forgotten that many years before the bear, when the girls were still feeding cabbage leaves to rabbits while small deer grazed nearby, they had promised to stay together and love each other always.

The boyfriend I had was from Chloe's college but in his final year. His hair was straight and long, and he liked to stroke cats. I went with him to rock concerts at the university and to exhibitions in the art gallery. Very soon after I met him I said, 'Excuse me but I am a virgin, and I am not going to have sex with you.' He said: 'Why do you say that as if it is a problem and as if you are ashamed? It is not something to be ashamed of.'

That was all he said, and it was very reassuring; comforting enough to sustain me as he knelt down in the street talking gently to mangy strays or stood for ages in front of old pictures making little sighing noises of appreciation. But although it was nice of him to say what he did, he was wrong about me. No, it was not that I was ashamed; I just wasn't saying the truth, which I sometimes thought he could probably tell somehow.

The boyfriend before had done this thing without my consent.

Oh yes, I had been lying on the bed with him, but not to have sex, and he knew that quite well, because he was not a new boyfriend, and we had talked all this over many times. So I was very shocked, when he forced his way into me. I struggled, and he withdrew. It took place very quickly, as if it was in a dream and was a mistake that was never meant to happen. Then I was bitter with sobs and insults and afterwards crying silently for a long time. I should have got up and walked away from him, but I didn't. This is strange. I was once in a car crash as well, and then afterwards, for months, I only felt safe driving with the very person who crashed the car. Anyway, I didn't stop going out with him, but I said, 'never again must you do this', and he didn't.

Because it wasn't supposed to happen, and because he was only inside me for a very short time, I thought at first that I was still completely myself. I had always believed that virginity was not really about not-having-sex and was more a state of being. Then I got frightened that I might be pregnant, and, of course, virgins don't (usually) get pregnant regardless of what state of being they are in. So, whatever a virgin might be, I quite clearly was not one and probably had never been. I felt very lost. That was what happened. That was when I started to tell other people that I was a virgin and to make a big thing of it – which I had never thought of doing before.

Janice also went around telling people that she was a virgin, but she did this mainly to spite her sisters who seemed to make not being a virgin anymore a very public sort of process. The one next to Janice was an outspoken virgin for a very long time, and her boyfriend said that she was armour-plated. Then one night at a party he came downstairs again and said 'I've found the tin-opener.' Janice's sister wasn't at all embarrassed. She came downstairs a bit later looking quite radiant, and the mood of the party improved considerably because of the happy consummation. How did she know that this was the right time? I wondered.

Now that Janice had left school I sometimes went with her into her world, but I had to wear disguises. In fact, Janice dressed me herself to make sure I wouldn't be found out and so that I would not disgrace her. To go to the nightclub with her and the other girls from her work, 16 had to be 21 and seductive. She bought me a long black skirt and a satin halter-neck top and kept them for me at her house, because I was forbidden. I think Janice liked me to come along with her; because she was confident she understood her place in the world, and I was very open to instruction.

Chloe also came to the nightclub when she wanted, if she felt like it, but she was an impossible novice. She was beautiful whatever she wore, but she liked to make believe, so she designed her own costumes and made them by hand from old dresses of her mother's, velvet curtains or from whatever she could find at the jumble sales. Once she made a long dress with a halter-neck top, and there was a brass chain threaded through like a necklace to hold it up. When she made a red velvet dress, the material was too thick for the sewing machine. She broke two needles and didn't finish sewing in time, and so we had to pin and stitch her into the dress to go out. Chloe's nightclub clothes were not the sort that Janice could complain about. They did not make her look childish or innocent, and they certainly did not make her look plain. But Janice could not help showing that she did not like them.

'You must realize you have to grow up', she told Chloe, 'boys feel uncomfortable with girls who dress and behave like you do.'

No not boys. It was girls who were frightened by Chloe, but not me.

I liked to go to the nightclub. If you arrived before 9.00 p.m., you could get in free (ladies), and if you brought vodka in your handbag, then you only needed to buy orange juice to drink. Janice provided cocktail cigarettes. She and I smoked the ones that matched our clothes early in the evening and the orange ones last when all the others were finished. At the nightclub Chloe only smoked 'Black Russians'.

There was a huge plastic palm tree that rose from the dance floor to the balcony where older couples ate chicken pieces served in white woven baskets and drank bottles of wine. We did not go to the balcony for chicken-in-a-basket. We went to look down on the dance floor to choose boys. This was where we decided which ones we were going to 'look then look away, look then look away' with for the evening. Boys were not frightening in this world at all. They were not serious. They were less real than the palm tree. If you caught one, he had to buy drinks for you and your friends all night (if they had not caught their own). I was very glad if I could get one, because Janice and Chloe were always having to pay for me, and it was nice if I could give them something back occasionally.

Some of these boys were really men. They were more generous with the drinks, but much more tiresome to get rid of. With boys it was quite simple. In the cold rain at 2.00 a.m. he would kiss you and say: 'I think you are really special and I really respect you. You are different from all the other girls. Can I see you tomorrow night?'

'Yes of course . . . but I really must go now.'

Goodbye for ever and thank you for all the sweet dancing.

Men, however, say: 'Can I give you a lift and I've got some drinks at my flat if you would like?'

Janice was my protector, and she would have to come and rescue me from these men. I must pretend to suddenly be very drunk, and she would loudly accuse my provider of trying to take advantage of me. She was my sensible friend, and she must take me home right away. Janice was very good at her part in this, and she sometimes managed to make the man feel so guilty he would order the taxi and pay for our escape.

It is funny when my mother first saw the one I brought in like a wild creature from the forest. She said, 'I see you have brought a real man home.' He had come to me from the other side of the world, and it was impossible to pretend that this was not a serious thing between us. That was when I got to be Snow White and marry the one who looked like a poor, starving bear from the dark wood. But was not I also Rose Red who had met this man because she liked to wander far and wide and would not stay at home? She made her own scarlet bed, and so now she would like to lie in it.

8

Little Flowers

Saint Francis was praying. He was kneeling on bare earth; a small piece of cleared ground in the forest on the plain. Assisi stood high above him among the mountains and its pink stones shone out as the early light touched them. But where Francis knelt it was still dark and cold and still night time. He prayed, and he beat his body with brambles, and blood flowed from his wounds, and he was scarred with their holy marks. The drops of blood fell on to the forest floor, and then there was a miracle. As the first sunlight reached the plain, as the first strong beam forced its way through the vaulted roof of the trees, there, on the forest floor, where there had been blood a flower sprang up. A flower bloomed from each drop of blood. These are the flowers that you can still see today growing in the courtyard; growing inside the railings in the church of St Mary and All the Angels.

The roof has been tiled, and the forest floor is marble now, but still they allow some of the light of heaven into the awful church, so that the roses can grow.

I had a child, but I did not bear him myself. As she had always loved us, my mother gave us this wonderful gift. She looked so tender and vulnerable that I forgave her for embarrassing me by becoming pregnant when I was already a teenager. She became round very quickly and held that full beauty for months. We knew that she would have to be delivered by the knife, because neither Ella nor I came from natural births. So my mother took us all to have a meal at the place with the dark polished tables and the silver, hissing coffee machine, and then we took her to the hospital to keep the night's vigil before the morning's ordeal.

My father sent us to bed early, but he was still awake downstairs with the light on when I went to the bathroom in the early morning. Long pale shafts of sunlight were slowly moving across the hill and into the woody valley where the double willow stands. Across from there it crept into the room I shared with Ella and where we had placed the new empty cot. This was the day when certainly the child would be born.

It was a school day, and so I was sat with Chloe and Janice, Kat and Sybil, in one of our secret places behind the tennis courts, when my father came to look for me. It was springtime with the cherry trees all in blossom. There were flowers everywhere. My father took me by the hand and told me about the baby boy with no wrinkles, because he had been lifted into life and did not have to push his way out through the steel muscle tunnel. The child was fair-haired but that may change. Already his eyes were dark and bright. My mother was very sore and tired, but she was happy. When he had left her, she was sleeping and the new baby was tucked into a white cradle and sleeping beside her.

In the evening Ella, Daddy and I went to the hospital, but that was a different world. All the beds, all the cradles and all the babies looked the same. Not only the baby but also my mother seemed unrelated to us. She was not ours again, until I came home from school a few days later to find her nestled in the big armchair in her new dressing gown. She had arrived home in the morning but had only just awoken from a deep sleep.

My mother said that she slept as she had never slept before; back in her own bed and away from all the crashing and noise in the hospital. It rained and that was the most lovely sound in her dreams; that and the sound of the baby breathing, curling his long lashes, opening and closing his sweet hands. Such a blessed baby he did not stir until she had finished with this good long sleep, and he was ready to take her breast and go back to sleep again.

'I am so happy', said my mother, 'to be back home with my family again. To sit here in my lovely pink dressing gown with white lace. Every woman should have a new dressing gown if she has to go into hospital to have a baby. Your father chose this one, and the flowered satin one when I had you and the blue and white one for Ella.'

Fine as a ball gown dressing gown and soft rain and my mother home again. I sat drinking tea to soothe the end of my schoolday headache. I sat at her feet, and she rested her hand lightly on my head. I was listening for the new baby to cry.

I didn't steal the baby from my mother. She said right away that the baby was not hers but ours. The baby was to share for us all. I just took her at her word.

On our sweet summer mornings the baby woke at 6 o'clock. I got up quickly and caught him to me. 'Darling, Darling, don't cry.' He was warm and damp in my arms, and his little cheeks were flushed. There was a bottle made up for him in the fridge, but it must be warmed up in a pan of water and then the drops of milk sprayed on to my arm to see that it was the right temperature. The milk must be the same heat as your own blood. The baby could not wait for his food. He tried to suck my arm, his own fist, the sleeve of his white flannel gown. When he could not find something to tug with his strong baby kisses, then he cried. It was impossible to tell him that it would not be long. That yesterday his milk was there, and it would be again today. The poor baby could not remember yesterday.

When the bottle was ready, I sat in the big armchair and held him tightly as he fed. He closed his eyes to suck the first great gulps, but then his anxiety left him and he sucked more quietly, looking around. When his eyes caught mine, he smiled and lost the teat from his mouth. I had to trace his lips with it and coax him to take it again: but then as soon as he did, I was smiling at him, and he smiled back at me and lost it once more. I gave him my little finger to curl his hand around, and I moved it away from him to test his grip. Babies are supposed to be able to support their whole weight with the grip of their tiny hands, but I do not know if this is true.

After the feeding was over, I changed his nappy and rubbed white cream into his skin. He was happy to lie there and kick for a while, but soon he was getting tired again. I pushed his pram into the garden; into the shade of the trees, because he liked to watch the leaves move and to reach out his hand and try to touch them. Then I walked in the garden holding my baby until he was almost asleep, before I put him into the soft nest. I liked him to sleep outside even if it was raining, and I had to put the hood up and the cover on. I liked to think of him breathing fresh air in and getting rosy cheeks. My mother said that was best. She said that she always used to push me into the garden when I was tiny, because I slept much better there.

A baby is a doorway into adult life.

Janice and I walked out to an old pub on the other side of the wood. It was early evening. The wood pigeons were still going about their noisy business, but we also spotted an owl sheltering close to the trunk of an oak tree waiting for the darkness. We took the baby with us, following the horses' paths. At this in-between time there was nobody in the bar. 'You don't mind if I bring my baby in for a little while, do you?' I asked the landlord. He smiled at the fresh young mother and said that it was a lovely evening for a walk and what a beautiful . . . is it a boy or a girl? . . . Oh, a boy.

Inside the pub it was cool, and we could smell the beer of last night's drinking. You can't smell this anymore when a pub begins to fill with people, because a new night has begun. We left when the night people begin to drift in. The sky turned from blue to indigo as we walked home light-headed through the damp, lush woods.

I found I could travel freely as long as I took the baby with me. Fewer questions would be asked. I took very good care of the little child, because he was my soul's desire. He slept in the bed that Janice shared with her sister, while we played cards, canasta and poker, downstairs. I was happy to have him near me, because this was my child, flesh of my flesh, of the same flesh as mine – more akin to me than to his parents. He was for me the child of promise. Born not from earthly union or by human will but sweet as a petal settled in my arms. A birth without any pain for me. My child was like the blossom on the blackthorn bush that appears unnaturally, while spring is in its earliest moments and it is almost still winter. There are no leaves to be seen and no sense of the sap singing in the branches; the petals unfold from the bare wood, the buds break out of the woody stems to flower. I was in my mothering blossom like the blackthorn bush before the natural time. I was just 15 years old and see me toss my baby in the air. Throw him away and catch, catch him again and hold him to me.

9

Fruit of the Spirit

'Midwinter Spring is its own season'.

In and out of time there are the births of the flesh and the births of the Spirit. You must learn that both of these are good fruits. You must then learn the harder lesson that these fruits all come from the same tree.

The Spirit and I had grown up closely together but drifted apart in the teenage years. This was not due to any quarrel but a natural divergence of different paths. When we came together again on the brink of adulthood, the relationship had benefited from this decent separation. No longer playmates we were free to fall in love. This love was a new birth.

Coming back from Chloe's I skirted down the path that followed the stream between the new houses and the wood. The stream was broad and shallow in some places with stepping-stones to cross by. In other places it ran slow and deep enough for us to crouch down in the water up to our shoulders. Chloe and I ducked and paddled and half swam in those shaded pools through all our childhood summers.

Out of a tangle of brambles growing by the stream sprang a hare. She sat on her hind legs and smelled the air, and then she began to run through the grass and on towards the horses' field. In her running sometimes she would leap in the air and twist her body. Dancing in the air, mad hare, springtime hare.

I thought about the hare, as I carried on walking along the path that separated the neat rows of new houses from the first silver birches of the wood. At this time I could still leap as she did, but there was a struggle going on inside. What was to become of me? Every day I felt I was becoming more choked and suffocated by the rough brambles. I felt a great yearning, and I felt as if I was not free.

I remembered an old song. He was a cavalier, and usually I supported the other side, but it was beautiful when he said to his beloved that he could not love her half so well if he did not love his honour more. This was what he said to her as he mounted his horse and went away to do battle. Sadly, she preferred the comfort of strong arms and a fire in the hearth to his fond farewell. But I could perfectly understand what he was saying: that you do not love someone well if they are what you love the most. Then love is too shallow. When people stopped believing in God, they started to have faith in love. But I was not destined for the movies. I did not believe in romantic love.

Nor did I truly believe in European culture. It is true that human beings are not small busy ants crawling between the sticks and fallen leaves. It is important that we can look up to where the light breaks through the branches. It is good that we refresh ourselves with the strong flow of words. Sometimes this runs full and deep, but it can also be a shallow babble. I was growing up. If I could refuse the first sweet seduction, then I could smile wisely upon this second.

Politics was more important. I had been drawn into the strong current that flowed between justice and injustice. Here was a torrent deep enough to bathe in. Why should this not be enough? I was not sure except that it seemed to me that politics would never break its own banks and overflow into the whole of life. Into the tenderest, most painful places. There is something about the world that cannot be reformed by hopeful politics. But politics at least did not fear death, or growing old, and was willing to toss the present in the air to catch the future. I decided to baptize myself in politics, but maybe there was something else?

Chloe and I would try almost anything. We sat in the roughest pubs and dodged the fights without spilling our beer. We swung very high on the children's swings. We visited an old lady every week who could not go out. She told us stories of wartime dances and poured us weak tea that tasted of dust. We went to the nightclub with the plastic palm tree growing from the dance floor to the balcony.

We went to a gospel meeting. There was no minister or preacher but people our own age who sang and talked. Chloe and I gave ourselves to the experience. The people spoke about how they had searched for freedom, and they promised us that they had found it. We could find it too if only we would dare to try. Chloe and I dared to try. We were not at all afraid to try a gamble.

They gave us Bibles, and we took them to the pub and read bits to each other. We had visions.

'I feel', said Chloe, 'as if I have been peeled. I feel tender but not sore. I feel smaller, but that all of me is sweet.'

'I feel', I said, 'that I understand something deeper than happiness. And I feel as if I have come out of a narrow space.'

The revival people left us after a few days, and this was painful. Chloe had wanted them to help her, because she was frightened of the person she was becoming; not truly herself but just the girl the wild boys wanted. By herself she tried to take in again deep gulps of freedom, but they had become for her great mouthfuls of warm milk. If it was not warm milk, it was the bitter bile of hell. She gagged on the drink. She did not want this at all. So back into the wild boys' arms. Back into the dance.

It was different for me. I had the tangle of morality at first and all the fear of hell; but somehow my first leap carried me over the barbed fences and over the flat and boring fields into the wilderness.

Sybil was distraught because of me. It was as if I had betrayed her. She tried to reason with me, and then she told me all her fears. That I would marry the first flat-footed man that came along speaking about Jesus. That all the promise of the future would evaporate into silliness and sweetness. She spent a lot of time, because she loved me, trying to help me see sense. She even asked her father to speak to me. He was very nice. He showed me a picture of a deep-eyed Russian icon and spoke of guerrilla priests in Latin America. I knew nothing of such things but felt they promised much. He was a true atheist, and so he understood the power of the Spirit. I felt he was a kindred mind and friend to me.

For this was a testing time.

Chloe and I could not speak, and Sybil had given up her persuasions for heavy sighs. She developed a great aversion to Gerard Manley Hopkins, who we were studying for A level, because he was a Jesuit. Janice was just completely oblivious to what was happening to me, and, to my surprise, it was Kat, always my enemy/friend, who was the best support. She was interested, and she did not mock. I began to appreciate the liberty and the amorality she had always had as her own element. These were not to be feared as I had feared them. I did not spend much time with Kat, but her calm curiosity helped me a lot, and I was grateful.

And meanwhile, despite all this disturbance, I was so in love.

I had a new way of being. I could lose all my sense of self and become a part of everything. The beck that flowed through the woods came out meekly just below the small railway station. On the wooden bridge I could look down at the water and be the water; see the small fishes and be the fishes. Watching a rush of people crossing I felt quite dizzy, because I realized that I could live their lives with all of them, share in them, be them. Not a thing was lost or forbidden to me.

A mother wheeled her sleeping toddler across the bridge in his pushchair. She was young, she had a heavy bag, and she had to go home, get the baby to bed and cook a meal before she could sit down. The baby was sleeping, and I could see the lines of tear marks on his face. The train journey had been too much, he was too tired. But sleep had come with the rhythm and the rocking. His little hands still held tightly to a teething ring. When they got home, he would awake crosser than ever and cry again. His mother would boil an egg for him and cut the toast into slices, and he would begin to calm down and then to laugh and smack his hands on his highchair as he ate. She would then wash him in the kitchen sink, and he would make splashes and point at the goldfish in a bowl on the windowsill. Later he would be dressed in pyjamas which were too long and needed to be rolled up around his ankles. Then his mother would make him the only bottle of milk he was allowed now he was a big boy. As soon as the last drop was finished, he would fall asleep.

The mother would then carry her heavy burden to the room, where thin cotton curtains closed out the summer day. I could be the mother and the baby, and I could go beyond both of them, go out through them. I was becoming intimate with the flesh of all that is.

To pray I walked through the woods, until I reached the bridge by the station, and I stood there to look at the water and be the water; and to look at the people and be the people. And I offered it all to the Spirit who offered it back to me with her light touch across the cheek and her soft laughter. This was a laughing that I could hear out loud and which often surprised me and made me laugh as I walked along the streets.

Such early love runs its course. Very gradually I came to the position where I knew the person I had become as a continuation of the person I was before. My friends were reassured when they saw I was not a stranger.

I was standing on a bridge that joined the worlds.

I liked to think of the generations of my family before me who had sat in squat, sooty, wooden-benched chapels and knew that, sitting right there, they were spanning to infinity.

though their newspaper wrapping, when he put the flowers on

10

Generation

Every Sunday my grandad came to our house for his dinner and his tea. In summer he always brought my mother a huge bunch of flowers wrapped in newspaper. You do not see bunches of flowers like these any more. Today you can buy five slender stems wrapped in cellophane at the supermarket. The florist displays strangely deformed parrot tulips, spotted orchids and indigo hyacinths tied with raffia – but we do not have flower bunches like those my grandfather brought. In these, enormous pink open roses bent their heavy heads and hollow-stemmed dahlias displayed their huge, spiked, battle helmets. There were Michaelmas daisies and chrysanthemums and these brought into the house the sharp smell of autumn. The daisies were mauve and purple and the chrysanthemums like dying orange suns.

When I heard his bus draw up near the double willow tree, I would run down the street to meet him. He allowed me to pretend to pull him up the hill and gave me his heavy bag to carry the last few yards down the garden path. When we got inside, he unloaded what he had brought. Water seeped through their newspaper wrapping, when he put the flowers on the table. Next to the flowers he placed the shoulder of mutton he had brought for our Sunday lunch. Blood seeped through its brown paper covering tied with string. I liked to poke the meat through its wrapping and feel the solid, lardy lump.

'Why do we always have to have mutton?' said my mother. 'It's so fatty. Why not chicken or beef?'

She sighed as she put the meat into the oven.

'And where can I put all these? Dahlias don't last. I've told you before . . . But they are beautiful.'

She sighed a deep sigh as she breathed in the chaotic smell and every vase in the house was put on the draining board for the arranging to take place.

Each Sunday after lunch my mother and my grandfather would have their quarrel. The starting point could be different, but the end place was always the same. Cromwell was a favourite place to begin. It was not the question of the monarchy or the terror in Ireland but the famous wart.

'Paint me wart and all he told the fancy painter who wanted to smooth him out and make him into a pretty picture not an honest straightforward man', said Joe.

'He was stubborn, obstinate and vain', said my mother. 'Any normal human being would have been grateful for that little touch of grace but not Cromwell. He thought he was God Almighty wart and all.'

There was a fundamental difference in the worldviews of my mother and her husband's father.

'You can do anything', said my grandad, 'if you have a book that sets out the instructions clearly.'

'Nonsense', said my mother.

'If the book is plain enough you can. When we were just married, your mother . . . '

'She wasn't my mother.'

He chose to ignore this plain statement of fact. He and his lost, lamented wife had become mother and father to the whole world.

'She said, "Joseph Walton, I want a French polished table". So I went to the library and borrowed a book and took our ordinary kitchen table and French polished it.'

'You can't make a silk purse out of a sow's ear.'

'Beautiful it was.'

'You couldn't paint the Sistine Chapel with instructions from a book. You couldn't write Wordsworth's poems . . . '

'Good fellow Wordsworth. Straightforward like Cromwell.'

GENERATION

'If Wordsworth had a wart, at least he had the courtesy not to inflict the knowledge of it upon generations yet unborn. At least he let his wart die with him.'

And my mother would go upstairs and read on her bed. My grandfather would tuck his trousers in his socks and go outside to dig our garden and fill it full of dahlias.

Joe was the first man I wanted to marry, and when he died, it was my first adult grief. On the train, summoned home, I wept loudly and all the other passengers in the carriage were silent, respecting my loss. He was the last of all my grandparents to die. They had died, and it was time for us to take our turns on the stage. To stand up and play our parts in turn.

My own parents do not say anything to me, but I know they wish to move on up to fill the vacant places, and I am stopping this happening. We all look younger than we are, because we are suspended between generations. Particularly I look younger than I am. I do not seem to change very much. I am a small dark person, and I do not have wrinkles; my face and body do not look worn. They are not worn, that is the reason why. Nor does Ella wish to have a child before I have a child. For the moment she is paused, she is waiting.

My friend Chloe has taken her seat among the mothers. She broke out and upwards for her own space and freedom, and because of this she has her own firm beliefs about people and children. There was a boy she loved. Before he became a wild boy, he had been her playmate and the boy next door. He thought that he was winning when she slept with him, but she was winning, because she had decided what she wanted. She got up from the bed and gave him a last kiss, but he did not treasure it. Then she went home and told her mother she was pregnant. She told her that very same day as soon as she came home. She didn't tell me until much later.

So now Chloe believes that if it is right within you, then it is right with your body and you conceive. She also believes that you are able to know the very minute that it happens. I have read many books, and so I have learned that sometimes it takes even more than two days before the sperm meets the egg. But Chloe knew, and her mother says that it is true, because she told her as soon as it happened.

If I ever get pregnant, I imagine that I will shine like the sun, but this is not what I have seen in life. Chloe went into eclipse. I was surprised, because before I even knew I noticed that she was wearing a scarf that looked wrong with her jacket. Then as the weeks wore on she just wore what was easiest, what her mother had washed, ironed and folded, and ugly shoes. She didn't wear clothes to hide her body or to display it either. The baby lay casually across her, and she didn't talk about it much.

Everybody else did. Her big sister and her mother were white-hot angry, because she would not tell them the name of the boy. Kat and Janice petted and cajoled and wheedled and were indignant, but she would not tell them either. I thought it could only have been her one-true-love, but I did not ask, and she did not tell. I only knew who the father was from the familiar face of the child.

The older generations attended the birth. They had gathered around, and we were kept away from it, because it was not seemly for us young women to be involved in this untimely thing. Her mother went to the hospital with her, and when I phoned to check that she was all right (the baby was early), it was an aged uncle, keeping vigil with his aged partner, who answered the phone. 'Chloe is in labour', he said as if it were a punishment. Nothing more.

That was at nearly midnight. At 6 o'clock in the morning he gave me the same message, and I felt as if Chloe had been removed from me to some lonely, toiling place where I could not reach her. A place with the ancestors.

It was a breech birth and difficult to bear. They numbed her then, and so it was just the long exhaustion and the feeling of her head being ten thousand miles away from her feet. Like Alice. The baby was not beautiful, and Chloe was grateful for this. It was an ordinary baby and hers alone. No one could want to steal this little red scrap away.

I went to see her in hospital and was shocked. She had no new dressing gown. Chloe was wearing a faded old nightie, and her face was blotchy from the hospital heat. She was sat in the day room smoking with some other mothers when I arrived. She would not have stood out from them. No one would have picked her out as special. I half imagined that she would have decorated her face. Painted it full of stripes and stars and flowers in celebration of her choice and achievement, but that was not her way anymore.

I took the baby in my arms, and I promised Chloe I would love him for her sake. She was quietly happy with the new child, but I wondered if she had noticed the dangerous beauty that was in his long fingers and thick lashes. There would be time for this to flower. Already he is a charming boy. I think that the wild boy who was his father has stamped his face and features, but that does not mean he will be like him. The patterns are more complicated than that.

The baby was born at the right time for Chloe to sit with him through the summer and feed him from her breasts. This was lovely to watch, but I was frightened that Chloe's absorption with the child did not stop when he fell asleep against her and she laid him in his cradle. She tucked her soul in beside him and returned soulless to talk and drink coffee.

She had a birthday, and I saved and bought her a sari of peacock blue and purple and violet and silver. I showed her how the woman in the shop had told me it should be worn, and she stood still as I folded and tucked and draped the glorious cloth around her. She enjoyed me dressing her. Moving her arms, winding around and around her. She loved the feel of the soft material on her arms, but she did not look long in the mirror. She sat all evening looking like a princess to please me, but I did not see her wear the beautiful cloth again, and she really was not interested in maiden games.

Chloe cried when she had to go back to working at her art, because she had to stop her milk and give her baby to her mother. The mother took the baby as if he were her own, and this made Chloe cry more. Nothing was as she wished.

'Be realistic. You have a child to support,' said the mother and the uncles.

'But I may never again have a baby at my breast, and these are precious days', said Chloe, but she did not have a choice. I know that Chloe's work was thought to be even better in those days after the baby was born, but that was because she worked hard, not because her soul was weaving light on to the paper. Her soul was held in warm sticky hands. The beautiful hands of her baby.

11

Growing Wild

In the city where I live now summer spills the people on to the pavement. Around my house the pavements are stained with beer and the blood and the vomit and the spit of summer days. And there is a wonderful smell in the air. I can smell it even above the smell of burning from the fire the children have made from rotten window frames and poured-on petrol. It is the smell of blossom; something like the perfume of the Linden trees on the European boulevard where we sit at cast iron tables and drink smoky beer. But it is stronger even and headier and mixes with its blossom sweetness the heavy sweetness of decay.

This is the scent of the hedges that have not been cut. The smell of the privet in blossom. Houses are hidden behind privet trees that do not neatly fringe low front walls but tower to shut out the light from the bedroom windows and block the pavement so that you must walk in the gutter and kick the cans that lie there. These are old trees with splintered trunks and dead branches that fall when the wind blows too hard, and then the children pick them up and bend them and break them and burn them for their own ends.

Chloe and I first met in a yellow classroom which had a picture of a girl in a yellow dress in a field of yellow corn on the wall. At first we liked the school. The teacher smiled at us. In the morning, while we were hanging up our coats, she would place a box of wooden blocks in the centre of each table. There were long orange sticks which were the number ten and purple sticks for eight. The sticks for five were bright pink; there were sweet blue blocks for two and little white cubes for one. When the blocks were put in lines, they turned into sums. We were always putting the blocks into lines and counting them up. The teacher said: 'You may use whichever colour you like as often as you like, but the blocks must always go in a line or back in their own spaces in the counting box.'

Chloe and I began to build. There was a crazy tower coming to life on the table. It was orange and blue and pink and white and we built it high. We took the blocks away from all the children on the table, and they watched us in silence. Then the teacher came and smack, smack, smack. Clip, clip, clip.

We wanted to be good children, but Chloe and I were victims of a misunderstanding. I read pages and pages of my reading book, and the teacher moved me up in the class to the table where the children have the most difficult work to do. This was fine and less boring, but the table was next to the Wendy House. I finished answering all the questions on the card and put my hand up for the teacher to come and see. She was busy, and so she did not come. I slipped off my seat and into the Wendy House. A big arm yanked me out again. Clip, clip, clip. I had to sit on the naughty boys' table, so the teacher could keep an eye on me. The only girl on the naughty boys' table. There was not much work to do, and we could give each other Chinese burns and tell jokes.

Dancing around the maypole was wonderful. The boys had blue ribbons and the girls' ribbons were white or red. Each ribbon had a loop at the end, so that you could slip your hand in. I was trying my best to be good and skip sweetly. The teacher was pleased with us; we had skipped in all the right paths and made a cobweb from all the single ribbons. There was a pause in the music, and then we skipped again; unweaving the web until all the strings were neatly stretched out again. I gave my ribbon to my partner, who took it back to the centre of the pole. Then he came back, faced me and bowed. I did a beautiful curtsey. This was really going well, and I loved it. I would be dancing in front of the parents on Saturday. Not every girl was chosen, because there were too many of us – but I was.

And then on Thursday Chloe came to school with a bandage on her knee. She could not dance and had to sit with a book in the hall, while we lucky children were dancing. Chloe was sad, and so I smiled and waved to cheer her up. The teacher said: 'If all you want to do is play around, there are plenty of others who are ready to take your place.' She made me give my ribbon to another girl and stand with my face towards the wall. She did not wish to see me cry.

It was because of all these misunderstandings that our fates became sealed. They will separate us, they will teach us, they will clip our wings, they will give us a clip around the ears; clip, clip, clip. They told us that they did not mean to stop us having our own interesting shapes, but that it was their job to do the shaping.

Two naughty girls said they could fight boys.

We stood back to back and linked our arms together. The boys were puzzled but decided to teach these two girls a lesson beneath the crab apple trees. There were four boys, and they came to grab us, but we kicked any boy who got near. We circled back to back, and the boys could not get near and they could not separate us. Through the long dinner playtime we stood together. At last all the boys fell on top of us, but when everyone managed to stand up again, our arms were still linked, and we were still kicking. The boys told the teachers that it was we two girls who started the fight. This was true, but teachers cannot punish two girls who are set upon by four boys. And so it was the boys who were punished, because we were learning how to escape.

I left Chloe and her baby for some weeks at the end of the summer to meet up with the revival people again and join them singing and preaching. We went to live in an old gospel hall in a Scottish city. The windows of the chapel were all close to the ceiling to let in the light but keep out the world. We had army camp beds, and the girls stretched washing lines across the rooms where we slept. The whisky distillery sent its vapours into the sweet morning air, and the people lived in tenements. There were stairs and closes, bin sheds, fire escapes, and drying greens. Everywhere was crowded, noisy and chaotic. Rosebay willow herbs grew between the paving stones and whole trees sprouted horizontal from broken drainpipes. The children walked through the streets with dirty faces, and no one called them to come and eat. No one called them to come on in now it's time you were in bed and long past your bedtime.

I had never been in a place like this, and at first I mistakenly thought that it was not the buildings, not the rusting fire escapes, but the people themselves who were falling into decay. I tried to tell them how they could become new and whole again. The people crowded into the halls to hear us – specially the children. They knew what to expect, because lots of revival people came to this place. It was susceptible to them. Every summer the people were saved, and nothing ever changed.

Some children told us that they wanted to join us. We welcomed them to come and eat with us and to share the services we had after the evening meal, before we went out on to the streets again. At first they wanted to learn the words of the songs we sang, so they could stand with us when we played music. Then they began to ask questions. I overheard the leader of our group talking with them:

'This is a wicked place, and the people here are a wicked people.'

When I heard him, I had that lurch in the stomach that tells me I am wrong. Whatever the message of the words I had been saying or the songs I had been singing, I did not truly believe that the people were wicked. In fact I had fallen in love with them.

I climbed up the back stairs to a place where a small door led out on to the flat roof of the Sunday school building. Everyone was looking for me, but they could not find me, so they left to do their preaching. I sat on the roof and watched the night fall on this beautiful place. I could see two young girls walking arm in arm, and I watched a boy practise goal scoring with a ball bounced against the wall again and again. A woman sat in a chair on her balcony with her feet up over the rails. The doors of the pub were open, and there streamed out golden light into the purple evening.

I blessed all I could see and offered it to the Spirit. She added her benediction and whispered to me that the crumbling world was beautiful and fruitful and just as it was intended to be.

'Can you bear this?'

'Yes, but with all the pain?'

'It is an agony', she said. 'But you must also worry about where there is no pain.'

Some of the people I knew as a child smelled of tea. In summer they went away to Christian guesthouses and drank tea there. On the last night there was always a concert in the lounge in which everything is good clean fun. The shadow of a person gets sawn in half behind a curtain, and a choir sings funny made-up songs to hymn tunes. Not too late the people go to bed, and no one tiptoes across the hall.

When I was little, I loved to go on these holidays too, and they are wonderful for small children, because there are carpet bowls and beetle drives and treasure hunts. I remember once one of the women guests had a beard, but she didn't seem to notice. Now I know that I would not wish my life to be lived according to kindly rules that suggest you wear your dressing gown and slippers if you are walking down the corridor to the bathroom. I would rather my breath smelled of wine than tea. I would rather someone knocked on my door in the darkness.

My love and I had sex in a foreign country. It was a country full of danger, and the police could be at the door. His bed was narrow, and there was a knife beneath his pillow. I cried out despite the danger. There was a gecko on the wall, but it did not like to move. Afterwards I fell asleep and he was still lying on me.

This is how I wish to live. This is how I live now.

12

Bindweed

The poet John Clare loved the common bindweed. The glorious convolvulus with its pure white flowers, more beauteous and fragile than those of the lily.

Of course, the poet was quite mad. Only a madman could fail to recognize his sweet convolvulus as a plant of easy virtue willing to attach herself to anything. She is also malicious. Given to catfights and unprovoked attacks upon her neighbours. She will crowd out those more cultivated than herself. She will steal and smother and strangle. You must root out this plant because it is neither peaceable nor productive. Convolvulus is a noxious weed.

'What is this?'

'It is convolvulus,' said my grandfather, tearing it down.

'I can't say convolvulus.'

'Tell your mother you can't say convolvulus.'

'I can't say convolvulus, Mummy.'

'Tell your daddy.'

'I can't say convolvulus, Daddy.'

'Will someone stop that child saying convolvulus, convolvulus, convolvulus . . .'

'Can we pick some convolvulus?'

'No, if you put even the tiniest shoot in your garden, it will get a hold.'

'Just the flowers?'

'But they have no stalks to hold them in a vase. See, they need the railings to support them. Look how their green stems wind round and round. The convolvulus has no strength of its own.'

'Why are you so frightened of it then?'

I do not think that things can be ordered so that everything grows rightly in its proper place.

When I was a student, I fell in love with a man who had a deep sense of holy vocation. He had a very strong effect on those around him. His words seemed to carry special significance, bear hidden meanings, people listened to him. He always appeared to be engaged in some serious inner struggle, even when he was just waiting in the line to buy his cigarettes and newspaper. Perhaps that was why his eyes were always red? Was it from weariness, or weeping, or gazing too long on invisible things?

These spiritual struggles were not without results; he was the voice of conscience and had separated the sheep from the goats. He could say with confidence what was right and what was wrong. He displayed the marks of his passion, and the air around him carried a crackling charge. But despite all his charisma there was a flaw in him. Sometimes it is necessary for the metal to be mixed with impurities if it is to survive the cooling process without cracking. In his case, the ore was a little too fine.

We both went to the political meetings, where we spoke in support of motions, voted on amendments and debated points of order. It was an exquisite mating game. Before he looked at me, I admired him. When he looked and looked away, followed me with his eyes, stood close without speaking to me . . . then I felt my own strength dwindle almost to nothing.

This man became my obsession. I began to dream about how I could help him in his future life. How he would be powerful and pour down fire, and how I should be with him through it all – although it would not be easy. Everyone could see him hold my hand and understand that we were together. I did not now myself speak at the meetings. His strength silenced me. I loved him to look at me, with his too bright, red-rimmed eyes, as if I was an appealing child. I was even content to hear him say, 'I can't see you tonight I've got something important to do.'

This love had no simple joy, only immense sensation. I no longer had a mind – I was all body. He had made this change in me. I was sitting in the Junior Common Room in the morning drinking coffee, and many men hovered around wishing to be with me, because I had become nothing more than a deep-throated flower.

But I did not care to attract them. I had no desire apart from him. He was my addiction but he had another obsession. As well as to the revolution we were making through our magic words (dialectical materialism, transitional demands, to secure for the workers by hand or by brain . . . the means of production, distribution and exchange); as well as to the strikers we stood with in the rain (warming our hands at their brazier and thinking that we would stay all day, but nothing happened so we left); as well as to these he had a commitment to the unborn child. He said that he was absolutely convinced (and always would be) that when cells began to multiply in the womb, there was human life and this life must be protected. I was not sure about this at all.

I had been thinking a lot about abortion, because my own mother was pregnant again, and I feared danger. She was all sensation, as I had become through love, because of this new child. She was too distracted to talk and looked as if she had a fever. They had already cut deep into her womb three times. This life was just too fragile, and I was sure that it would break. Maybe it could break her? Perhaps it would be born broken?

But my boyfriend said that all was as it should be. The right thing was growing in the right place.

Then my mother started to bleed, and they put her to bed. She felt as if people were poking sharp sticks into every part of her body, and so an ambulance was called.

'I want the baby', she said.

'But the baby is dead', they replied, 'we must suck it all away, pluck out every tiny bit, and then you will heal again.'

I was summoned to travel from the university and go to my sad home. To go with my sad father to the hospital with flowers. My mother's skin was translucent. She was drugged and weak. I told her little bits of loving things, and I tried to describe the man who had become the centre of my life. She held on tightly to my hand trying to feel baby fingers.

I went back to the university. That evening my boyfriend was busy chairing a meeting called to protect the unborn child. A woman had come from the national organization to speak. There would be trouble, but that would not worry him. It would confirm the importance of his mission. I was too sick to go. I thought, surely he will knock on my door just as soon as the meeting is finished and stay to mourn with me the death of this unborn baby.

By midnight he had not come, and naked and weeping I crawled into my bed. At that point, I did not want to hold this man in my arms. I wanted to kill him. I would have liked to see him crushed and bleeding and broken. I wanted to tell him that he was able to care for things that were invisible and could not be touched but that he was not able to give the green touch of love where that touch was needed. In the night my mind kept waking me. It woke me with a vision of me pushing this man under a car, hitting him with a stone, plunging skewers into his eyes.

He did not come in the morning either, and I was too weak to seek him out. By the evening I had begun to rage again inside, and I showered and dressed with all my nicest clothes and red, red lipstick. He was sat in the Union Bar, and sweet and sour I went to sit beside him. He finished the important thing that he was saying, and then turned to look at me – with approval, because I was pretty and smart.

'You should have been there last night. It was terrific. And the woman who spoke; she was amazing. I stayed up till 3 talking with her.'

'My mother.'

'Yes, how is your mother?'

'She is broken.'

He paused. I had not given the right answer.

'She'll be all right. My mother had four miscarriages, and she's all right.'

Now his expression had changed. He was looking at me disappointed, as if I had failed an important test.

Sadly and kindly he explained to me a week later that we were not really compatible. There was something important missing in our relationship. It was not going to survive.

I went down to the Union Bar that evening and saw a student from the year below me standing there. He was one of the ones who had become fascinated by me because of the new scent that hung in the air around me. He was kind and he was handsome. He had no magic words, no sacred causes or great ideals, but he was a human being and he would help me.

'Come with me', I said to him. 'If you don't mind, please stay in my room with me until tomorrow morning.'

We did not sleep. He held me and told me little stories about his schooldays and pets and sailing in his uncle's boat. And he sang in a band, so he sang to me as well. Sometimes we just lay quietly. He whispered he had never held someone like me in his arms before. When I was crying, he made a joke, and I had to laugh, because he looked so eager, and he had freckles and dimples and open, honest eyes.

We got up early and sat in the kitchen of the student residences. The other women students looked at my young man, as they prepared their breakfasts. They were thinking that I had seduced him for my own desires. I did not care if they thought this. I wanted them to think this. I wanted them to believe that I walked out of the arms of a man who was too pure in his loving, and had drawn to myself, for my own pleasure, this lovely companion. I hoped they could see that I was free of my obsession. They could see that I was happy. I did truly feel light and happy. And so they would speak of my shallowness and my easy sexuality. Fine. Good. Let them speak loudly then.

The man with red-rimmed eyes stopped me as I crossed the quad.

'I did not know you had something else going,' he said. For once he seemed to be really looking at me as if there might be something going on behind my eyes. I wanted to say that he was the only one I could ever love; but I knew it was quite dead. It had been sick from the moment it came into being and was now all over. I just did not speak to this man. I had decided to stay with a clear-eyed honest person who was younger than me until I was healed. He played pinball not politics and his skill and intuition meant he was very good at this indeed. More important, he was happy to take the green life I offered him for all that it was not quite love.

With him I was always glad and calm. My voice returned and my reason. I liked to sit reading, drinking coffee, looking on while he played pinball with his friends in the common room. I was proud of him. He was funny and bright. But one day I noticed the way that he was looking at me was changing. He had become accustomed to my eyes upon him across the room, and he smiled, expecting a look in return that signalled 'we are together despite all these other people, and we are happy'.

Well, I was happy, but I was not content, and it was very wrong what I was doing. I was letting him begin to love me, but I was not properly loving him in return. I was the destroyer this time and was holding in my grasp something precious that I would only waste or ruin. Also I was unfaithful, because while he was thinking of nights together in the smoky bar and the kisses later, I was thinking of a long journey all alone. I had begun to make secret plans to leave him. It was time for me to go.

I was travelling to a very cruel land for serious reasons. I wanted to test myself and all the beliefs I had. I wanted to see how people lived when the fences were destroyed and the little foxes had broken into the vineyard. I was not going to fall in love or to have children. I was not going to build a house to inhabit. I would dwell secure in my own strong soul and take the power of the Spirit for my shelter.

So I had to take a coach to London from where I must also take a plane to Johannesburg.

Chloe came to see me off. I cried for what she had. I would never have lived all my life in one place in the way it is natural to live. I left my home to go preaching, to go to university, and now I was leaving again. I would not be raising a child in the place where I was raised. I knew the consequences of my actions. I could not rely upon roots sunk deep in my native soil for support. I was always going to be the one who was the stranger and must bend her slim, green stem round others.

And Chloe cried for what I had. My winding strength. The way that I could be broken and still put out new shoots from within myself.

We cried for our friendship and this long separation.

13

Green Stones

The teacher said to bring a shoebox to school but we did not have one. My grandfather always took them to store his dahlia tubers in through the winter. My father had a box that his new shirt had come in which was big enough but not as sturdy and not the same shape. I was worried. But it turned out the shape did not matter. We were making moss gardens. We gathered cushions of moss and filled the bottom of the box with a deep, luxurious layer. In this we stuck bare twigs which had small, pink tissue blossoms. You could use pebbles too and make silver paper streams or mirror lakes if you wanted. The moss was an impossible green. No real grass could match it and it made a spring garden out of nothing.

My friend and I sat in the sweet sunshine on the daisy-covered grass in Canongate churchyard. It was Saturday morning, and we had newspapers and milky lattes. Just feet away from us tourists were toiling up the Royal Mile, but we were alone in this green place with the famous dead. Just to impress them I said: 'Jacques Maritain believed that if you admit the existence of the tiniest speck of moss clinging to a gravestone then life has overwhelmed you and you have fallen into the terrifying hands that made us all.'

My good friend looked into her wax paper cup, and then she said, 'I have always thought that God was like a huge, lazy, lovely, red-haired woman. Her place is a mess. She leaves her coffee cups unwashed and spots of mould start to form in the dregs and traces. Each cup contains a cosmos to itself. She has this effect on things. She isn't tidy enough to stop them growing.'

My friend was right I think. First there is decay, dust, dirt. This makes a place for the spores to settle. But this was not something I understood then, when I got down from the plane and looked around me at a bright, new world.

In this whole continent I did not know one person, and it was a marvellous freedom. Because I was not known, had no roots, I could pretend I was not flesh but air. Here I had a delicious, empty purity. Often it was as if there was no me at all and only the serious needs of this serious country.

At first I had lodgings in a long narrow room in a family house. The room was white, and there was a dark little wooden bed, with starched white sheets and a white counterpane at one end and a desk at the other. My Bible was on the bedside table. In the evenings I closed my door and sat in here with the windows open to hear the frogs and the crickets. I worked hard at my desk taking notes of all I had seen.

I read newspapers and cut out bits to file. I wrote down tables of statistics noting infant mortality, malaria, and TB. I studied philosophy and wrote my diary. I liked this serious person I was playing. She had taken her vows and was dedicated like a nun. But then I went to visit. I stayed in another house. There was no place for me there. I had to sleep in the bed of whichever person was away that night or in the space that was left when two people shared one bed. There were no clean sheets. I was sleeping in the hollows other bodies had left in the mattress, in rooms where clothes other people had worn were scattered on the floor and where the cigarettes they had smoked were still in the ashtray.

In this house everyone would gather in the kitchen to drink strong tea when they got home from the meetings they had been to or the bars they were drinking in. It was the dirtiest kitchen in the world, and it had cockroaches hidden in it. If I walked into this room in the middle of the night, the floor, the table, the walls would be black and rustling with cockroaches, but if I switched on the light in two seconds they would be gone. Back into the cupboards. Back into the drawers. People sat in this kitchen who must not be seen anywhere else. They arrived without notice and were gone again without anyone commenting. Those were things we did not talk about. Everything else but not that. Perhaps they had slipped into one of the beds in this big house and would emerge later in someone's old dressing gown, or perhaps they had slipped away across the border.

One night there was a priest sitting at the table. He brought a five-litre flagon of rough red wine which we drank from the chipped and stained tea mugs. We talked and laughed, and then he took photos from his inside pocket to pass around. He had with him photos of people who had been killed in custody. How did he get these, and what was he going to do with them? Don't ask. Just look. I had to gaze on the faces of people who had been hanged and see the way their tongues had swollen and darkened in their mouths as if they had been gagged with the very part of them that was made for speaking. I had to see the dark bloody bruises on their eyelids and imagine how it had been when the pressure had pushed eyeballs from their sockets. My own eyes felt as if they had been branded and that the negatives of these images would dance across my eyelids each time I closed my eyes.

This table was our altar.

One hot day I brought home a huge, sweet watermelon and cut it into irregular pieces with the bread knife so everyone could have a slice.

Here we all sat together making sweet potato curry and brandy punch for the Christmas party. We had drunk most of the punch before the party started, and I danced very close with many of the men before morning. That night I did not sleep in a bed at all but on the large sofa in the neglected lounge. Wrapped up next to me in the heavy curtains we had taken down from their rails was a man with long, dark curly hair and deep brown eyes. We had come together in this ugly and painful place which was more alive than anywhere I had ever been before. But was the excitement I was now caught up in something I could approve of when so many people were dying? How could there be so much rampant, careless life?

This man was offering me love, and I had to choose whether I would go back to my white room and continue to believe that this was a bleak, pure country or stay in his arms and acknowledge this was a fertile place of crimson joy.

14

Lily

> The modest Rose puts forth a thorn,
> The humble sheep a threat'ning horn:
> While the Lily white shall in love delight,
> Nor a thorn nor a threat stain her beauty bright.

In the year Ella was born it was the coldest winter for 20 years. My mother was in labour for two days before they decided to operate. The baby was wee and delicate, and everyone was delighted with her. She was beautiful with dark lashes and quiet dreaming to herself in her cradle. But I could not hold her or watch her sleeping. I had to be sent away and was not allowed to be with her, because I had mumps and I was infectious. I had to stay with my grandparents and receive visits from my father. He came late, because I was the last thing in his busy day. I was already tucked up under the pink eiderdown in my grandparents' bed. By the light from the hall he showed me in his wallet a clip of my mother's hair, a clip of my dark brown hair and a new clip of jet-black hair. So tiny and with so much hair.

For nearly two weeks I was kept away from my mother, and the new baby was her only child. I was shy to enter my unfamiliar home again. The big pram blocked the hall, and it was so warm, because my father had borrowed all sorts of heaters from our neighbours: paraffin heaters, gas heaters and one-bar electric fires. The air was heavy with heat and fumes.

I loved the baby. I loved her with every bit of me. At night I crept out of bed and went over to the cot to watch her sleeping. Many times my father had to pick up a five-year-old girl who had fallen asleep with her head against the wooden bars. And yet she had destroyed my world. My mother was distant; she was either weeping or looking into the sky blue eyes of another child – my eyes are cloud grey.

I had become a jealous little girl. My sister had a white plastic dog on wheels, and I took it from her and pulled it behind me wherever I went. When we went to the seaside bed and breakfast, I demanded to sleep in the cot that had been set out for her, while Ella slept in the soft-quilted bed that should have been for me.

When I met Chloe at school, I found some relief from all these pains. I told her that I had cruel parents. I said they fed me on bread without butter and that when I got home from school, they sent me straight to bed, where I had to stay until morning. Chloe felt very sorry for me and stole food and brought it to me in her satchel. She stole red apples and Battenberg cake for me to eat at playtime.

So Chloe became my best friend, and we held hands and walked everywhere together. When we sat down, I leant my head upon her shoulder, but I was jealous of Chloe too. She played in the garden of the girl across the road after school, and she seemed happy to mix with the other children her parents invited around because they did not like me very much.

Chloe's mother asked, 'Who shall we invite on your birthday?'

'I only want my best friend.'

'Well then, that's all you shall have. Just "my best friend".'

I wore a paper hat and sat opposite Chloe at her birthday party, and it was very solemn as we ate our jelly with mandarin oranges.

Because I was jealous of Chloe's affection, I was always looking for ways to test her.

'Don't go home. Stay at my house for tea.'

Chloe would be punished for neglecting the food prepared for her at home. But she did not argue, and she stayed. She would always prove her love, but no proof satisfied; or ever satisfies.

In ancient Greece Euripides wrote a play about the unhappy love of a jealous woman. Medea was the strong wife of Jason. By her cleverness and cunning she had won the Golden Fleece and fame and honour for him. How he loved her when they were on the run, but now they had settled in Corinth he had slipped her arms and gone to the bed of a princess.

'How unhappy are we women', said Medea. 'As children we are kept within our walled gardens. No one teaches us the arts of love. What skills we will need to survive in the houses of our husbands. No one tells us of the dangers of love.'

'No one tells us of the dangers of love', said Medea. She had grown up in a walled garden and loved with terrible innocence. When this was betrayed, the Lily became a poisonous flower. Medea killed her children. Because I was not innocent, my love could not be so terrible like Medea's. It had firm and open petals. There was a faint fresh smell about it like briar roses – but so many thorns. If this man were going to come to me, I would need to make some way through the thorns that had become almost impenetrable since the days of my 'holy affair'. I would have to prepare myself like a bride.

I slept a lot, because this preparation took all my inner energy. It seemed I had never been so tired. Right through the middle of the day I slept and woke without a headache or the feeling of wasted time. I was lying asleep at the heart of this busy beehive house in which so much happened. The house was a focus point of strange power in this enchanted country, and in its shelter lay a girl/woman who slept curled-up throughout the day. Although so sleepy I was quite aware of what was happening. I knew that because of what was taking place nothing would be the same again, because the whole world was involved in my chrysalis transformation. I was gripped by a terrible nostalgia. The rain would never feel as it had done before on my bare skin. The pavements would be different to walk on. The colours would shift their places in the spectrum. Not only would the world be strange, it would also be dangerous. By surrendering my thorns I was putting myself at risk.

If there came a bang at the door in the night and the police burst into the house, they would find me where I shouldn't be. They would catch me completely defenceless. There was sweat in the tender place below my stomach which came from the touching of our flesh as we slept.

When we made love, it was as if we were lying naked in the street, because they were watching. I knew there were no places they could not see. In the house itself there had to be enemies as well as friends. There was nothing we whispered that was not recorded.

Well, as the defences were useless I had to live without them. I could learn to live without them. I could also learn to be dumb blind; to move in a world where I did not see and had learned not to question, 'Who is that?', 'What is that?', 'What did that person say to you?'

There is one rule. If you do not know you must not ask.

But if you cannot see or hear, what is left is touch and taste. I touched not only with my outer skin. I touched my friends through those inner nerves that are usually protected. I tasted salt and sweet as I had never tasted them before.

I had not thought you could take a holiday during the war, but we were offered one. We were lent a house that overlooked the ocean. The reflection of light on the waves marked the light walls of our cottage, and they were rippled like the sand. The sea roared all the time. After breakfast with strong coffee we would set out to walk along the beach, and although it was the same walk every day, it seemed different because we found new treasures each time. Our small sea-house was a long way from the main road, and we rarely met any other people. We wrote love messages in the sand and left them there for the waves to wash away. Once we wrote forbidden slogans in huge letters but quickly rubbed these out again with a stick in case there was an enemy hidden behind the sand dunes. In the evening, our cheeks red from the fresh air and all our limbs heavy, we sat by the fire. We ate fish fried with spices and hot chillies and drank red wine.

On our last evening there was a full moon, and we could not stay indoors while the sea was so silver. In a place where the vegetation met the sand we made love. It was sandy and shivery and noisy from the sea. Woody roots poked into my back. How could two people open themselves up so much to each other? I thought. This is so dangerous I might die. I was sick with love.

We had a plan, and it seemed very simple. We had decided that we would join our love to the passion of the country and that our invisible child would be the better future. That was what we had decided as we walked by the sea.

But the times were difficult, and we knew that we had to be wise as serpents as well as innocent like doves. What is important to recognize is not only whether you are strong enough in yourself to bear the burden of the day but whether you can also carry the added weight of your responsibility for others. If you are becoming overwhelmed, then you are not the only one who is in danger.

We had talked about it and said 'there is work that can be done even outside the country and this work is important too'. And so we decided to leave for a while – although this was not meant to be for ever. It seems we lost our way by mistake. Staying away just that little too long and then finding that our return was forbidden. It was an accidental exile – we had removed ourselves, packing our own bags and buying our own tickets. It was as if we had organized our own banishment to save any inconvenience.

Standing with comrades at the rally in the chilly London church hall I felt as if I could no longer properly sing the freedom songs that rose and fell around us, so beautiful. Among the real exiles I sometimes felt ashamed and uneasy, as if we had been easily tricked into a betrayal we could have avoided if we had been more wakeful. I don't know. They were difficult times.

15

Bearing Fruit

What is the saddest thing I have seen in the garden?

I planted an apple tree and it opened its buds to make leaves. These were fresh and shiny but the tree was sick and so the leaves fell. Below the first buds were second buds which were the plant's defence if the first leaves failed. The apple tree burst into leaf again but not as thick, not as green, were these sparse leaves. They were good enough, however, to make food, to take a breath, and yet there was something very wrong and so these leaves fell also.

By now it was autumn, and through the cold winter the tree rested. It had made buds for the spring. When April came and all the other trees were not only putting forth leaves but also in blossom, this tree uncurled its few sparse leaves. But the shoots were black at the tips and down the central vein the rottenness spread. Each leaf was torn at its heart and soon dropped.

There was no energy for new leaves, but the tree still lived. If I scratched the bark, I could see green where the sap still flowed. But as summer stretched on and the other trees swelled with fruit the bark on my tree shrank. The branches no longer had the green sap of life. Only the trunk showed green. By autumn time that too had shrunk, and there was only rotten yellow beneath its skin and orange mould in spots. The tree had to be quickly dug up and burned. No other fruit tree should be planted where it stood for a whole generation.

Savage garden.

All of us children had rabbits. Mine lived for eight years, even though we fed her on oats mixed with tea leaves which was what my grandad insisted rabbits liked best. She was white with dark brown circles around deep eyes which showed amber lights.

My little brother had two sweet twin rabbits: their fur was black and chocolate brown. My brother's rabbits were the tamest of all because he played with them so often. They would sit happily in his arms. He smuggled them into the house and fed them ginger biscuits in his bedroom.

One night when everyone was asleep, some people came into the garden and opened the hutches of my brother's pets. They opened the doors and let their big dogs off the lead. They tossed and tore the soft, gentle creatures. My brother went in the morning to feed his rabbits and found blood and fur.

My brother, my little child, I am so sorry that this is how the world is, and you have had to see how the door posts have been daubed with innocent blood.

Why does it happen this way?

That was a summer in which it seemed each day brought more bad news. People we knew were imprisoned, hands that we had held were blown off by parcel bombs. A friend was shot and bled to death in a car park. But we wore an invisible mark that only the guilty wear. This kept us safe when we should not have been safe. Yet riding the strong currents of pain we learned to comfort each other and to kiss again without feeling that each tenderness was a token of betrayal. This was our resistance too. To live life together to the full in the place where we found ourselves now. Not only to live but to make our dwelling and to plant orchards and tend vineyards. We were in hope for a child, and I wanted to make love all the time. In sex I had visions of harvest and plenty, and I was the golden goddess Circe.

But then nothing happened. I did not get pregnant. Still there was the excitement in sex, but it was like Berlin before the war. The wrong sort of gaiety and sex, because death is close and the frenzy cannot last. I was becoming exhausted with all this trying, and my life being so red and black instead of all the good colours with green and yellow.

I hated going to the doctor. I hated sitting there, pale, and confessing I could not conceive. On his desk were pictures of his children. He was kind, but this was not a kind situation. He told me what to do, but I did not like his instructions. I did not like to spy on my body and discover its secrets. I did not want to know the temperature of my blood. I did not wish to say, 'Ah today the mucus is clear and stringy and can stretch between the fingers. Today the mucus is dense and cloudy. Maybe there will be rain.'

My partner must be tested too. His sperm looked good and healthy, and they could see them, when they looked, like sea creatures living in the pools and crevices around my cervix. This lack of a conception was a puzzle. So then they had to try and gain a confession from me about what might be wrong.

'Some women', said the specialist gently, 'bleed on the inside when they should let their blood flow away outside. This makes pain and scarring. Do you have this?'

I thought of the summer of the kissing game and of Chloe and Sean together. I thought of the love I had for the man with a holy mission. Maybe its dead remains were not all sucked away? If some was left to go bad inside me, perhaps it had caused the living tissue to harden and scar? But I did not think that this was true. I bled when I was hurt. I bled a lot, but then it stopped and I was healed. There really was no bitterness or badness left. The blood that I shed marked my passage to maturity that's all. Aches like these are not to be regretted.

'Some other women', said the man in his very calm voice that does not judge, 'have grown things within themselves that should not be there. These growths are sometimes not painful or visible, but they do prevent conception.'

What had grown that was not a baby? What had grown within me that had left no room for my child? I lived with my brain and my imagination. I liked to sit with the artists and gaze through the open windows. I had a greater love than the loves of the body. Simone de Beauvoir filled her life without giving birth. She believed that she was a complete woman, but perhaps she was just a woman living in a hotel room with no space for a child.

This man was trying to weaken me, and I had to be on my guard against him. He was like the kind interrogator probing for my most vulnerable point. The prisoner is more likely to yield to his compassion than to shouting or beating. But I knew that what he was saying was not true. Children like to play in the wide-open spaces of the mind. The home of my soul could be a bright nursery. It was not a dead and dusty library. It was a picture house.

And still this man kept on trying. 'The body, like all living things, keeps its own cycles. In most normal women these are regular. They mark the very pattern of her life. We can see from your charts and temperature graphs that there may be some problem here. There may be something unseasonable about you.'

I winced because he might have touched the spot. Had I not always tried to grow without waiting? Did I not always steal kisses? Out of season I held a baby in my arms and worse than that I was not its real mother. When I fell in love it was in a forbidden place. What was secret was unnaturally public and no normal woman would be so shameless as to make love with so many eyes upon her. I thought I could break the rules and take a holiday in the war. I did not think as I took him in my arms, in the place where the dark line of rainforest met whiteness of the sand, about what the consequences of my actions would be. No wonder I could not now root a baby in my womb.

I had to summon all my strength to resist these charges. My answer to the interrogator was this:

'A woman's life does run in cycles. These are not only the cycles of the moon and blood. There are also cycles of generation, of friendship and the building and decay of the places that we make upon the earth. But you know, you have made it your business to know, and you do know in your heart, that when conception occurs it is not a continuation of these cycles. It is a break and a moving forward. Not a circle but a steep upward climb.

'Because I have been a creative person many times, I have broken the circle of my life. I have not despised the regular rhythms; I have just travelled through them and attempted the sharp climb higher. You cannot accuse me of this. Men always want women to be fertile but not potent. I will not stand accused because of my strong powers.'

There are always tests for those who are reluctant to confess. Tests that will reveal exactly how things really stand, if they themselves are unwilling or unable to tell. The specialist said that this was just a small operation, and the cut would be made at the tummy button, so there would be no visible scar. I could go to the hospital in the morning, and if all went well, I would be back in my home the next day. My arms were black and blue from the blood tests, and my mind was bruised by the dreadful questions. I thought there might be some peace in the test. At least I would be innocent in sleep and could not lie to spite myself.

They made the small cut and shone light on all my secret places.

They found nothing unnatural at all.

The specialist was upset, because he had tried to help me and failed. The interrogator regretted that there was no repentance from error and the victim herself longed to be able to enter into his approval and would have given her body to be burned if only it could satisfy him. Nobody could tell the reason why, but one clear fact remained. I did not conceive. I was a barren woman.

'Perhaps', the interrogator said very sadly, 'this is how you wish it to be. Maybe for some reason you are resisting what is normal for women, and you do not wish to bear a child at all?'

This was the very worst temptation he could utter! It was certainly true that my first true love had not been for any man but for the Spirit. People say the Spirit is a jealous lover and that she burns away with fire all the dying and decaying things that are needed for life to take root. Everyone knows the awful purity of the Spirit. She is like acid rain that leaves the lakes like crystal so that you can see right to the bottom.

Sensing victory he smiled as he said, 'You are a woman who has dedicated herself to the Spirit and the body that you wear is just a husk or a shell. Inside are not bones but fire.'

It seemed to be very dark, but I could see that this was now the time before dawn. Only those who have not known the Spirit as I have known her could be deceived by those words.

Yes, the Spirit can burn with fire, but I saw her swinging her hips as she walked the city street. I watched her laughing and joining in the singing; her light shining out of the open pub door into the summer night. She was very close when I lay sleeping beside my love in a foreign land where there was a gecko on the wall that did not like to move. Only those who have not met the Spirit think that she lives above the earth of sweat and dust. I have been intimate with the Spirit, and I know what I am saying is true.

'You are quite wrong', I tell him, 'so let me be now.'

His faint voice went on talking. 'We can do things that used to be impossible. There are still many things that could be tried. You can change your perceptions. You do not have to think of yourself as infertile. To us you are still a potential mother . . . '

As he talked, I drew close to me in my mind a story that defied him. It was an old story of the master carpenter Shi and how he was taught a lesson. The revered old man was walking with his apprentice when they passed a huge cork-oak tree that was a shrine to the god of soil. It was so huge that beneath its shade could shelter several thousand oxen and its branches could have been fashioned into a whole fleet of sailing ships. People stopped to wonder at its size but the wise carpenter Shi walked past it. When he had finished marvelling, the apprentice ran to his master and asked, 'Why did you not take an axe to the tree? Its branches would provide enough timber to last for both our lifetimes.'

'Foolish boy', said the carpenter, 'can't you see that the wood is rotten? If you made a boat of it then it would sink. If you made a door it would ooze sap. If you made a pillar it would be infested by worms. It is a tree with bad timber and is of no use. That is why it has grown so large.'

That night the cork-oak tree appeared to the carpenter in his dreams. 'What are you comparing me with?' it said. 'With the fine grained trees that produce quinces, pears and cherries? Their usefulness leads to their exhaustion. I, on the other hand, have been dedicated to uselessness for many years. I am now so useless I have achieved the highest honour and become sacred to the god of growing things. Moreover, there is much in common between us. You are a weak and unsound man approaching death. Who are you to call my wood rotten?'

16

The Flowering Rod

Eve works in the garden. Everything bursts its bounds here. There is too much fruit to gather. What does not fall directly into the hand must be left to rot on the tree. Eve is pregnant and lazy, but the garden must be tended. It has to be worked even if that means just pruning what has grown too quickly so that it can bear even more in the years to come. Eve swells in the opulent garden and remembers the command:

> All the earth is yours
> So work and feed
> Fill your swelling stomach
> Eat and breed.

What a vulgar little rhyme. How very like God to be prosaic. She rephrases the injunction:

> Be fruitful and multiply
> Fill the earth and subdue it.

Much more satisfactory . . .

Everything has its mirror image. Eve spelled backwards is Eve.
   Eve is a small dark person who is not pregnant. She sits still and the cells within her do not multiply. She does not experience the cancer of birth. She does not tend or tame the earth, because she knows that to subdue anything will in the end

destroy it. Besides which Eve is not safe to work in a walled garden. This is a very wild place.

I sat with Chloe on the wall beside the railway track. I was telling her about the interesting things I had read in the magazines my mother kept in the airing cupboard.

'Did you know the average married couple make love three times a week?'

'No', shrieked Chloe, 'I don't believe it.'

Her denials are drowned by the roar of the train. She is very upset.

'I am sure my parents only made love two times. Once for me and once for my sister!'

In those terrifying days of her innocence Chloe insistently rejected a world of constant coupling and intercourse. Perhaps that is now my destiny also? To protest against a world that claims to be governed according to the laws of nurture and procreation.

I was Eve working in the garden tying in the raspberry canes, and my hands and my lips were stained by mulberries too soft and sweet to gather. I wanted to bear good fruit, but something happened in the night, and there was blood on the grass in the morning and nothing would grow any more.

So now I am that other Eve. A small, dark person who lives by her wits in the savage garden. You have been told that the universe is a place of constant growth and regeneration. I am compelled to contradict you and say that it is a barren, wasted place. For all the things that grow there are partners in things that never came into being. I am their mother, and even if they are forgotten, I shall remember them. I am their witness.

Once the Spirit said to me, 'See how much is given.'

Now she whispers of what has been denied. So much has been denied. How many cold stars, how many frozen deep or burning hot stars, for just this one green earth? And yet without them what motion, what fire or ice, except that which has been borrowed?

Perhaps one day she will lead me out of here, show me a place to clamber out beneath the barbed wire fence and inherit a green and golden portion. In dreams sometimes I do seem to taste her milk and honey. But when awake, I am captured by the strange beauty of this wilderness. See how sweetly blow my poppies. How brightly they flower even in the churned-up earth, growing among the twisted metal, from the patch of earth that is stained dark. There are wild roses too. Wreaths and wreaths of briars.

How beautifully grows the bindweed. It grows between the links of the wire mesh fence. It grows right to the top of the wire mesh fence. The only flowers they can see when they press their cheeks to the fence which is too high to be climbed and there is no escape from the beams of the arching lights.

Mine are the only flowers that can grow in such a place. They are necessary.

And there in the corner blooms a fragment of the true cross. Blossoms coming straight out from the bare wood. I confess that it does not grow very strongly but it is a miracle that it grows at all. You will have been told not to believe that this is the cross upon which the Saviour hung. To you it seems a false and pagan relic. I am not so sure. To me it is a mysterious thing, and it certainly is alive – though in a way I cannot understand. Standing close I can see that it is stained with blood. Perhaps this is holy blood? And perhaps also it is the blood of all those who treasured it, kissed it, fought over it, haggled for it, traded it, stole it, passed it from hand to hand and touched it in the hope of a healing.

I suppose that some of them were children.

The blossoms have a lovely scent.

Questions for Reading Groups Using this Book

1. What role does the symbolism of gardens, plants and growing things play in the text?
2. The narrator's friends and family are of key importance in this work. What struck you most about these relationships?
3. Is everyday family life a place of epiphanies for you? Or does spiritual experience happen when the mundane is escaped for a while?
4. What have you learned about infertility from reading this work?
5. How do you feel about including sexuality in a work of spiritual writing?
6. This is a story told in a female voice and from a woman's perspective. How does the narrator's gender shape her spiritual journey? Could a man follow a similar path?
7. Does the author make convincing links between politics and spirituality or do they remain very separate areas of concern?
8. The author has said that this work helped her to understand how and why she became a theologian. Can you identify how your own experiences have contributed to your spiritual identity?
9. Where precisely is the spiritual in this life writing?
10. What do you think about the ending? Does the book finish on a positive note?

QUESTIONS FOR READING GROUPS USING THIS BOOK

11. Could this book be described as a parable (a story with a strong but not straightforward message)? If so, what meaning would you draw from it?
12. What do you like about the book and what do you find less helpful?
13. If you were writing a book that described your own spiritual awakening would there be a transcendent divine within it? If so, what names would you use for God?
14. What title would you give your own spiritual biography?

Resources for Writers

Books on Writing for Professional Development, Reflective Practice and Personal Wellbeing

Bolton, Gillie, 2014, *The Writers Key: Introducing Creative Solutions for Life*, London and Philadelphia: Jessica Kingsley

Bolton, Gillie, 2005, *Reflective Practice: Writing and Professional Development*, London: Sage

Bolton, Gillie, Victoria Field and Kate Thompson (eds), 2006, *Writing Works: A Resource Handbook for Therapeutic Writing Workshops and Activities*, London and Philadelphia: Jessica Kingsley

Ellis, Carolyn, 2004, *The Autoethnographic I: A Methodological Novel about Autoethnography*, New York: Altamira Press

Hunt, Celia, 2000, *Therapeutic Dimensions of Autobiography and Creative Writing Activities*, London and Philadelphia: Jessica Kingsley

Hunt, Celia, and Fiona Sampson, 1998, *The Self on the Page: Theory and Practice of Creative Writing in Personal Development*, London and Philadelphia: Jessica Kingsley

Muncey, Tessa, 2010, *Creating Autoethnographies*, London: Sage

Books on Theological Reflection

Graham, Elaine, Heather Walton and Frances Ward, 2005, *Theological Reflection* Methods, London: SCM Press

Klug, Ron, 2002, *How to Keep a Spiritual Journal: A Guide to Journal Keeping for Inner Growth and Personal Discovery*, Minneapolis, Augsburg Fortress

Paterson, Michael, and Jessica Rose, *Enriching Ministry: Pastoral Supervision in Practice*, London: SCM Press

Walton, Heather, 2014, *Writing Methods in Theological Reflection*, London: SCM Press

Ward, Frances, 2005, *Lifelong Learning: Theological Education and Supervision*, London: SCM Press

Weisel, Elie and Beale, Timothy, 2000, *Strange Fire: Reading the Bible after the Holocaust*, Sheffield: Sheffield Academic Press

Wolfteich, Claire, 2002, *Navigating New Terrain: Work and Women's Spiritual Lives*, Mahwah, New Jersey: Paulist Press

Life Writing and Writers Lives: A Personal Selection

Cixous, Hélène, 1993, *Three Steps on the Ladder of Writing*, New York: Columbia University Press

Dillard, Annie, 1990, *The Writing Life*, New York: Harper Collins

Hillesum, Etty, 1999 (1981), *An Interrupted Life: The Diaries and Letters of Etty Hillesum*, translated by Arnold Pomerans, London: Persephone Books

Smart, Elizabeth, 1991, *The Assumption of the Rogues and Rascals*, London: Paladin

Selected Academic Resources

Anderson, Linda, 2004, *Autobiography*, London and New York: Routledge

Eakin, Paul John (ed.), 2004, *The Ethics of Life Writing*, Ithaca and London: Cornell University Press

Kauser G. Thomas and Joseph, Fichtelberg, eds. *True Relations: Essays on Autobiography and the Postmodern*, Westport CT: Greenwood Press

Lee, Hermoine, 2005, *Body Parts: Essays in Life Writing*, London: Chatto and Windus

Leigh, David, 2000, *Circuitous Journeys: Modern Spiritual Autobiography*, Fordham University Press

Ricoeur, Paul, 1991, *A Ricoeur Reader: Reflection and Imagination*, edited by Mario Valde, Hemel Hempstead: Harvester Wheatsheaf

Walton, Heather, 2007, *Imagining Theology: Women, Writing and God*, London: T and T Clark

Journals

Spiritus: A Journal of Christian Spirituality: John Hopkins University Press

Literature and Theology: Oxford University Press

Reflective Practice: Taylor and Francis

Life Writing: Taylor and Francis